Multiple Choice Questions
for
Intermediate Economics

Second Edition

J. HARVEY

Macmillan Education

First published 1972
Reprinted 1974
Second Edition 1978

Published by
MACMILLAN EDUCATION LIMITED
*Houndmills Basingstoke Hampshire RG21 2XS
and London
Associated companies in Delhi Dublin
Hong Kong Johannesburg Lagos Melbourne
New York Singapore and Tokyo*

Printed in Great Britain by
BUTLER & TANNER LTD
Frome and London

British Library Cataloguing in Publication Data

Harvey, Jack, b.1892
Multiple choice questions for intermediate
economics. 2nd ed.
1. Economics—Examinations, questions, etc.
I. Title
330: 076   HB171.5

ISBN 0–333–23547–9

CONTENTS

PREFACE

READERS of *Intermediate Economics* will already have had experience of testing their understanding of the basic concepts and their ability to apply them through the questions at the end of each chapter.

This book sets similar questions in 'multiple choice' form. Its aims are:

(1) to provide a quick test of the understanding of basic principles;
(2) to highlight the salient points for revision purposes;
(3) to give experience in answering this type of question which now figures prominently in the papers set by certain GCE examining boards.

In order to save space, detailed instructions have not been given with every question. Where there is no introduction to the question, the student should simply select the choice which seems to him correct or most nearly correct.

PREFACE TO THE SECOND EDITION

This edition:
  (1) updates certain questions;
  (2) includes questions on the EEC (Section 24);
  (3) introduces new multiple choice questions of the 'assertion/ reason' type.

These assertion/reason questions are marked with an asterisk*.
The following directions apply to all such questions. Select:
  a. if both statements are true and the second statement is a correct explanation of the first statement;
  b. if both statements are true but the second statement is NOT a correct explanation of the first statement;
  c. if the first statement is true but the second statement is false;
  d. if the first statement is false but the second statement is true.

	First statement	Second statement	
DIRECTIONS SUMMARISED			
a.	True	True	Second statement is a correct explanation of the first
b.	True	True	Second statement is NOT a correct explanation of the first
c.	True	False	
d.	False	True	

1 WHAT ECONOMICS IS ABOUT

1 The total amount of goods and services produced in the UK today is:

 a. just sufficient to satisfy people's wants
 b. unlimited
 c. determined by nature and outside the influence of man
 d. less than people want

2 'Economising' can best be described as allocating limited resources in order to:

 a. secure the greatest possible satisfaction from them
 b. satisfy as many wants as possible
 c. satisfy the most important wants first
 d. obtain the same satisfaction from the last unit of each commodity bought

3 The opportunity cost of a good is:

 a. what it originally cost to buy
 b. how much it would be worth to its owner
 c. the most desirable alternative which has to be foregone in order to retain it
 d. what goods it can be exchanged for

4 In an economy where there is full employment, the government should increase its spending on education if:

 a. there would be benefits to society as a whole from additional education
 b. private enterprise is unlikely to provide additional education
 c. the benefit from extra education is greater than the cost of going without any other goods or services
 d. the total benefit obtained from education as a whole exceeds its cost

5 Which of the following would be of *least* concern to an economist?

    a. the possible effects on the car industry of an increase in car exports

    b. the likely demand for cars in a year's time

    c. the effect of a change in purchase tax on the demand for cars

    d. how a car engine works

6 I An economic good is one which can be obtained only by giving something in exchange for it.

II All goods which are useful are economic goods.

III All goods whose supply is limited are economic goods.

Which of the above statements is true?

    a. I only   *b.* II and III

    c. I and III   *d.* II only

7 Which one of the following statements is true?

    a. economics is concerned with the morality of given ends

    b. economics can never be regarded as a science because it is impossible for it to investigate and test by means of controlled experiment

    c. economic principles are usually derived from assumptions which are simplifications of what occurs in real life

    d. economists can always give a unique answer as to what policy is desirable

8 The primary concern of economic theory is:

    a. to advise a businessman on running his firm

    b. to establish economic laws to explain past behaviour

    c. to show where the government has made mistakes in regulating the economy

    d. to explain from given data what economic events are likely to follow

9 Under the private enterprise system, the economic problem of 'what goods' shall be produced is solved primarily by:

    a. people advertising their wants

    b. direction by the government

    c. the pattern of consumers' spending

    d. people producing directly to satisfy their own wants

10 Under the private enterprise system, the economic problem of 'who shall receive the goods produced' is solved primarily by:

    a. distributing income according to the needs of individual consumers

    b. rationing by the government

    c. consumers bidding up the prices of those goods they are anxious to buy, and refusing to bid for those goods they do not want

    d. firms bidding for factor services whose owners receive an income to buy goods

11 The distribution of goods by the price system is defective when:

    a. factors of production are mobile

    b. no allowance is made for social costs and social benefits

    c. there is a high degree of competition between producers in the economy

    d. there is full employment

12 One advantage of the free price mechanism for allocating resources in an economy is that it:

    a. avoids unemployment

    b. reduces inequality in incomes

    c. affords the fullest opportunity for individuals to indicate their preferences for goods within the limits of their spending power

    d. always results in goods being produced at the lowest possible cost

	First statement	*Second statement*	
13*	In the UK, people's standard of living is limited because goods are scarce.	Scarcity of goods in the UK is caused by the inequality of incomes.	C
14*	The USA and the USSR do not differ in the fundamental economic problems they have to face.	The USA and the USSR differ in the ways they go about solving their economic problems.	b

2 PRICE IN THE FREE MARKET

15 In economics, a 'market' is defined as:

   a. any place where tangible goods are bought and sold
   b. a specific place where buyers and sellers meet
   c. all those buyers and sellers who influence the price of a good
   d. the business centre of a community

16 Which of the following markets is likely to be the *least* perfect?

   a. the Stock Exchange
   b. the foreign exchange market
   c. the second-hand furniture market
   d. the Rubber Exchange

The following diagram refers to questions 17 and 18.

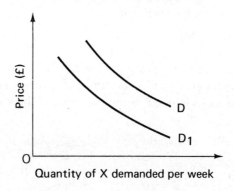

17 The demand curve D shows that:

   a. more X is demanded as its price rises
   b. as more X is demanded, the price rises
   c. more X is demanded as its price falls
   d. the only factor which affects demand is price

18 A shift in the demand curve from D to D_1 would be likely to result from:

   a. a fall in the price of a close substitute for X

   b. a fall in the price of a good which is complementary to X

   c. a rise in the incomes of people who buy X

   d. a subsidy to the consumers of X

19 An increase in the number of houses demanded at present prices is, other things being equal, likely to result from:

   I An increase in the number of marriages.

   II A rise in real income.

   III A rise in the rate of interest charged to borrowers by building societies.

   IV A net fall in the population through emigration.

Which of the above alternatives is consistent with the statement?

   a. I and II   *b.* I and III

   c. I and IV   *d.* II and IV

The following diagram refers to questions 20 and 21. It shows supply curves for different periods of time, 1 and 2.

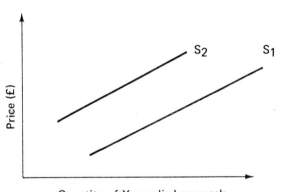

Quantity of X supplied per week

20 The supply curve S_1 shows that:

   a. more X is supplied to the market as its price falls

   b. as more X is supplied to the market, the price falls

   c. more X is supplied to the market as its price rises

   d. the only factor which affects the supply of X is price

21   A shift in the supply curve from S_1 to S_2 would be most likely to result from:

   a.   a fall in the cost of raw materials
   b.   an improvement in methods of producing X
   c.   a government subsidy to producers of X
   d.   a rise in the wages of workers producing X

The following information and choices refer to questions 22 to 26. On the diagram, D and S represent the original demand and supply curves respectively for colour television sets:

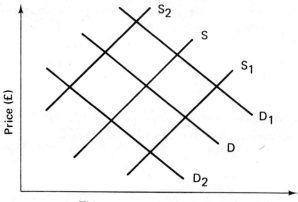

TV sets demanded and supplied

  a. D_1 *b.* D_2 *c.* S_1 *d.* S_2
Indicate which one of the above choices would depict the following changes:

22   A rise in people's income.   *a*

23   A considerable rise in the cost of a colour television receiving licence.   *b*

24   Improved techniques for producing colour TV sets.   *c*

25   A substantial rise in the wage-rates of workers making colour TV sets.   *d*

26   The BBC conducts a campaign advertising the advantages of colour TV.   *a*

27   A market is said to be in equilibrium when:

a. the number of buyers equals the number of sellers
b. sellers are satisfied with the price they have obtained for their goods
c. at the ruling market price buyers do not wish to add to the amount of the good which they already have
d. at the current market price, the amount which buyers want to buy just equals the amount which sellers want to sell

28   An increase in the demand for and a decrease in the supply of a commodity will:

a. increase price and increase the quantity exchanged
b. increase price and decrease the quantity exchanged
c. increase price but leave the quantity exchanged as it was
d. increase price but leave it impossible to say the effect on the quantity exchanged without more information

The following diagram refers to questions 29 to 34.

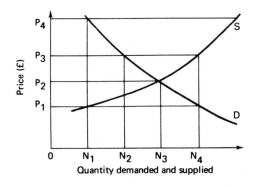

The following choices refer to questions 29 to 31.

a. OP$_1$ *b.* OP$_2$
c. OP$_3$ *d.* OP$_4$

29   What is the equilibrium price? *b*

30   At what price would supply exceed demand by N$_2$N$_4$?   *C*

31 At what price would demand exceed supply by $N_1 N_4$? *a*

The following choices refer to questions 32 to 34.
  a. ON_1 *b.* ON_2
  c. ON_3 *d.* ON_4

32 What quantity is demanded at the equilibrium price? *c*

33 What quantity will be demanded if the government fixes a maximum price of OP_1? *d*

34 What quantity will be supplied if the government fixes a maximum price of OP_1? *a*

The following information and choices refer to questions 35 to 37. The demand and supply schedules refer to the market for tennis rackets.

Price per tennis racket (£)	Demand (per month)	Supply (per month)
5	450	650
4	500	600
3	550	550
2	600	500

  a. 5   *b.* 4
  c. 3   *d.* 2

35 What would be the equilibrium free market price (in £)? *c*

36 What would be the price (in £) if demand increased by 100 tennis rackets at all prices? *b*

37 What would be the price (in £) if, on the original demand schedule, the government imposed a tax of £2 per tennis racket on buyers? *b*

The following diagram refers to questions 38 to 41. It is assumed that the demand for wheat remains constant but supply conditions change from the base period S_1 as shown by the curves S_2 in period 2 and S_3 in period 3. The government has a stockpile which it uses to stabilise the price of wheat at OP_1.

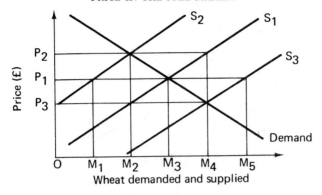

The following choices refer to questions 38 and 39.
 a. $+M_2M_4$ b. $+M_3M_5$
 c. $-M_1M_3$ d. $-M_2M_3$

38 What will be the change in the stockpile in period 2?

39 What will be the change in the stockpile in period 3?

The following choices refer to questions 40 and 41.
 a. $OP_1 \times OM_1$ b. $OP_1 \times OM_5$
 c. $OP_2 \times OM_2$ d. $OP_3 \times OM_4$

40 What will be the revenue of farmers in period 2?

41 What will be the revenue of farmers in period 3?

	First statement	*Second statement*
42*	The second-hand book market tends to be an imperfect market.	People do not have perfect knowledge of the prices at which similar second-hand books are selling in different shops, jumble sales and street stalls.
43*	Other things being equal, if the price of coffee rises, the demand for tea is likely to increase.	Tea is a substitute for coffee.

3 A FURTHER LOOK AT DEMAND

44 By saying a good has utility, an economist means:
  a. it is very useful
  b. something has to be given up in order to possess it
  c. it is not socially or morally undesirable
  d. it has the power to satisfy a want

45 The marginal utility which a consumer derives from a good is:
  a. the utility he derives from a particular unit
  b. the change in his total utility as a result of adding one unit to his stock of a good
  c. the change in total utility resulting from a change in the price of a good
  d. the change in his total utility when he buys extra units of a good

46 According to the law of diminishing utility:
  a. total utility of a good diminishes as the amount of it possessed increases
  b. a good becomes less useful as the amount of it possessed increases
  c. the utility derived from any given addition to a consumer's supply of a good will eventually decline as the amount he possesses increases
  d. the utility derived from successive additions to a consumer's supply of a good will eventually decrease

47 A housewife is said to be in equilibrium in the spending of her income when she:
  a. could not increase total satisfaction by buying more of one good and less of another
  b. obtains the same satisfaction from every penny she spends
  c. obtains equal utility from each good she buys
  d. obtains equal utility from the last unit of each good bought

48 A consumer spends his total income on two goods X and Y. He will be in equilibrium when:

    a. the utility of the last unit he buys of X equals the utility of the last unit he buys of Y

    b. the utility derived from the total quantity of X bought equals the utility derived from the total quantity of Y bought

    c. the ratio of the marginal utilities of X and Y is equal to the ratio of their respective prices

    d. the marginal utilities of X and Y are equal

49 When the price of a good falls:

    a. the consumer's equilibrium position is not disturbed

    b. the utility derived from the last unit of the good bought will fall

    c. more utility is now derived from the last penny spent on the good

    d. less utility is now derived from the last penny spent on the good

50 The reason why a consumer buys more of a good when the utility from the last penny spent on it increases is because:

    a. its price has fallen

    b. he has allocated a given amount of expenditure to the purchase of that good

    c. by so doing he will lower the utility of the last penny spent on that good so that it once more equals the utility obtained from the last penny spent on other goods

    d. other goods are relatively more expensive now

The following information and choices refer to questions 51 and 52.

Price ($£$ per unit)	Units of X demanded per week
8	200
7	300
6	600

a. 2   *b.* 3

c. 4   *d.* 5

51   What is the elasticity of demand for X when price falls from £8 to £7?

52   What is the elasticity of demand for X when price rises from £6 to £7?

The following diagram and choices refer to questions 53 and 54.

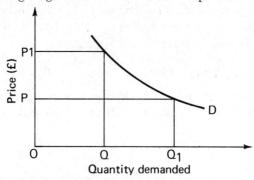

$$a.\ \frac{QQ^1}{OQ^1} \div \frac{PP^1}{OP} \qquad\qquad b.\ \frac{QQ^1}{OQ} \div \frac{PP^1}{OP}$$

$$c.\ \frac{QQ^1}{OQ} \div \frac{PP^1}{OP^1} \qquad\qquad d.\ \frac{QQ^1}{OQ^1} \div \frac{PP^1}{OP^1}$$

53   Which one of the above measures elasticity of demand when the price rises from OP to OP_1?

54   Which one of the above measures elasticity of demand when the price falls from OP_1 to OP?

55   Which one of the following statements is true?

a. if the total outlay on a good increases when price falls, demand is inelastic

b. if the total outlay on a good decreases when price falls, demand is elastic

c. if the total outlay on a good increases when price rises, demand is inelastic

d. if the total outlay on a good remains constant when price falls, demand is elastic

56 All the following would tend to make for a high rather than a low price elasticity of demand *except*:

   a. a large number of substitutes

   b. a small proportion of income spent on the good

   c. a large number of alternative uses for the good

   d. a large number of people cannot quite afford the good at its present price

57 The price of a commodity is £4 per unit and at this price 20 units are demanded. If price elasticity of demand is 2, how many would be demanded if the price fell to £3 per unit?

   a. 24   *b.* 26

   c. 28   *d.* 30

58 Where the demand curve is a downward-sloping straight line, price elasticity of demand:

   a. decreases as price falls

   b. increases as price falls

   c. is constant at all prices

   d. is equal to unity at all prices

59 Income elasticity of demand is:

   a. $\dfrac{\text{the proportionate change in quantity demanded}}{\text{the proportionate change in price}}$

   b. $\dfrac{\text{the proportionate change in income}}{\text{the proportionate change in price}}$

   c. $\dfrac{\text{the proportionate change in quantity demanded}}{\text{the proportionate change in income}}$

   d. none of the above

The following information and choices refer to questions 60 to 62. You are given the following information about commodity X:

Price (£)	Demand (units per week)	Supply (units per week)
4	60	140
3	80	120
2	100	100
1	120	80

   a. 4   *b.* 3

   c. 2   *d.* 1

60   What is the equilibrium price?

61   If incomes increase by 25 per cent and the income elasticity of demand is 2 at all prices, what will be the new price (in £)?

62   If wages now rise so that supply is reduced by 50 at all prices what will be the equilibrium price (in £)?

63   If the demand for commodity X is:

   a. absolutely inelastic, a change in the conditions of supply will have no effect on the price of X

   b. elastic, a small rise in price leads to a smaller proportionate fall in the quantity of X demanded

   c. infinitely elastic, a change in the conditions of supply will have no effect on the price of X

   d. infinitely elastic, a change in the price of X will have no effect on the quantity of X bought and sold on the market

64   When the demand for agricultural products is inelastic:

   a. a price rise results in a fall in farmers' receipts

   b. a price fall results in a fall in farmers' receipts

   c. a price fall results in a rise in farmers' receipts

   d. a price rise makes no difference to farmers' incomes

The following information refers to questions 65 and 66. The owner of a seaside car-park wishes to make as much profit as possible. His sole expense is one car-park attendant who is always on duty during the opening hours. He can cope with the maximum number of cars that the car-park will hold. The owner estimates the demand schedule as follows:

Price (pence)	Number of cars parking
50	60
40	80
30	100
20	120

65   What price will he charge?

   a. 50p   *b.* 40p

   c. 30p   *d.* 20p

66 Which of the following statements is correct?

a. at prices below 40p demand is elastic

b. at prices above 40p demand is inelastic

c. at prices above 40p demand is elastic

d. since a given price rise always produces a given rise in the quantity demanded, elasticity of demand equals one

67 In a certain town there are two restaurants, X and Y. X doubles its prices, but Y's prices remain unchanged. How will this affect people's total spending on restaurant meals in the town?

a. it would increase spending in Y, but might decrease or increase spending in X

b. it would increase spending in X and increase spending in Y

c. it would increase spending in X, but might decrease or increase spending in Y

d. it would increase spending in Y, but spending in X will remain constant

68 British Rail are considering altering fares. Which one of the following conditions would be certain to increase profitability:

a. an increase in fares where demand is elastic

b. an increase in fares where demand is inelastic

c. a decrease in fares where demand is elastic

d. a decrease in fares where demand is inelastic

First statement	*Second statement*
69* The consumer is in equilibrium when the possible total satisfaction he can obtain from his limited income is at a maximum.	Total satisfaction from a given income is maximised when it cannot be increased by spending a little less on one good and a little more on another.

4 SUPPLY: BRINGING TOGETHER THE FACTORS OF PRODUCTION

70 Which one of the following could best be regarded as an 'entrepreneur'?

  a. a bank manager
  b. a football club manager
  c. a salesgirl in a dress shop
  d. a rag and bone merchant

The following choices refer to the policy of a public company and apply to questions 71 to 74.

  a. building a new factory
  b. holding increased stocks
  c. maintaining sales in a credit squeeze
  d. increasing the rate of dividend to shareholders

71 Which one of the above would most likely be financed by current profits?

72 Which one of the above would most likely be financed by an overdraft from a commercial bank?

73 Which one of the above would most likely be financed by an issue of debentures?

74 Which one of the above would most likely be financed by increased trade credit?

75 A public company wishing to raise capital to build an additional £500,000 factory would most likely make use of the services of:

  a. the Stock Exchange
  b. a joint stock bank
  c. a finance company
  d. the Industrial and Commercial Finance Corporation

The following choices refer to questions 76 to 79.

   a. a sole trader
   b. a private company
   c. a public company
   d. a co-operative society

76 Which one may have its shares dealt in on the Stock Exchange?   C

77 Which one pays a dividend according to the value of goods purchased from it by the shareholder?   d

78 Which suffers the disadvantage of unlimited liability?   a

79 Which can raise capital by making a public issue by prospectus?   C

80 Which one of the following statements applies to the ordinary shareholders of a company?

   a. they receive their dividend even when profits are insufficient to pay the debenture-holders their interest
   b. they have no voting rights as regards the policy of the company
   c. they cannot force the company into liquidation
   d. they have unlimited liability for the debts of the company

The following choices refer to questions 81 to 86.

   a. debentures
   b. ordinary shares
   c. convertible unsecured loan stock
   d. cumulative preference shares

81 Which one carries the greatest voting rights as to the policy of the company?   b

82 Which receives a fixed rate of interest by way of return but still incorporates a hedge against inflation?   c

83 Which would have to be decreased proportionately in order to increase the gearing of the company?   b

84 Which would be repaid first if the company closed down?   a

85   Which would be the best to hold if there were a considerable increase in profits?

86   Which affords the greatest hedge against inflation?

87   Which of the following statements is *false*?

The Stock Exchange:

    a. provides a market in old securities
    b. advertises security prices
    c. examines the standing of companies seeking a quotation
    d. provides funds for new companies requiring capital

88   Which one of the following businesses would be most likely to reduce transport costs by moving its centre of producing from the market for its product to the source of its raw materials?

    a. a firm producing pig-iron
    b. a manufacturer of furniture
    c. a brewery
    d. a printing firm

89   Where weight is gained in the course of production, a firm will tend:

    a. to produce near its market
    b. to produce near its sources of raw materials
    c. to be indifferent where it produces
    d. to go to a Development Area in order to obtain tax concessions

90   A 'footloose' industry is one which:

    a. has no transport costs
    b. incurs higher transport costs if it is near its sources of raw materials rather than its market
    c. incurs higher transport costs if it is near its market rather than its sources of raw materials
    d. is not bound by considerations of transport costs to be either near its sources of raw materials or its main market

91 Improved heating techniques and the use of inferior ores has led to the following changes in the approximate raw materials necessary to produce 1 ton of pig iron:

	1950 (tons)	1970 (tons)
coal	$1\frac{3}{4}$	$1\frac{1}{2}$
iron ore	2	4
limestone	$\frac{1}{4}$	$\frac{1}{4}$

These changes have induced new iron firms to establish themselves:
  a. nearer to the coalfields
  b. in Development Areas
  c. where existing firms are already producing
  d. nearer the iron ore fields

The following information and choices refer to questions 92 and 93. By working 40 hours per week, Smith can make 6 hockey sticks *or* 4 fishing rods, and B can make 10 hockey sticks *or* 4 fishing rods. In the market, a fishing rod exchanges for a hockey stick.
  a. 8 hockey sticks + 4 fishing rods
  b. 6 hockey sticks + 6 fishing rods
  c. 4 hockey sticks + 6 fishing rods
  d. 10 hockey sticks + 4 fishing rods

92 What is the greatest production when there is no specialisation?

93 What is the greatest production when specialisation takes place?

94 Which one of the following reasons for a fall in costs is an external economy of scale?
  a. firms employ more specialised equipment
  b. the government builds roads to serve a developing industrial district
  c. an efficiency expert shows how labour can be better employed within the firm
  d. a large order for products is obtained

95 'Diminishing returns' refers to an eventual fall in:
  a. the average product of the variable factor
  b. the marginal product of the fixed factor
  c. the total product
  d. the marginal product of the variable factor

96 For the law of diminishing returns to apply, an essential condition is:

    a. all factors of production must be variable
    b. at least one factor must be fixed
    c. it must be possible to buy all factors under conditions of perfect competition
    d. units of the variable factor must be of differing qualities

The following information and choices refer to questions 97 to 99. The table shows the output of commodity X as successive workers are added to a fixed amount of land and capital:

Number of workers	11	12	13	14	15	16
Total output (units of X)	242	288	338	378	403	416

    a. 12 workers   *b.* 13 workers
    c. 14 workers   *d.* 15 workers

97 At what level of employment does the marginal physical product become a maximum?

98 At what level of employment does the average physical product become a maximum?

99 At what level of employment do diminishing returns set in?

100 A farmer working under conditions of perfect competition decides that his profit-maximising output is 96 tons of potatoes. The prices of labour and land are such that his optimum combination to produce this output is 4 acres of land with 8 men. The price of land is £30 per acre per year and the marginal product of the 4th acre is 5 tons. The marginal product of the 8th man is 20 tons. How much per year does each worker cost?

    a. £120   *b.* £160
    c. £200   *d.* £240

First statement	*Second statement*
101* An author who is paid on a royalty basis is an entrepreneur.	The entrepreneur bears the risk of producing for an uncertain demand.

102* The sole trader is a common form of entrepreneurial organisation.

The sole trader enjoys limited liability. ⊂

103* Prices of shares on the Stock Exchange fluctuate.

The demand for and the supply of shares on the Stock Exchange can change from one day to another. α

104* People buy ordinary shares of a company because they offer a hedge against inflation.

Dividends on ordinary shares normally increase as money profits rise. α

105* Specially designed doors would be made by a local joiner, whereas standard-sized doors would be mass-produced by firms like Magnet Joinery Ltd.

The extent to which the division of labour can be applied in the production of a good may be limited by the size of the market for that good. α

106* Even if two people are equally good at producing a certain article, it may still be profitable to specialise.

Practice in doing the same job increases dexterity. α

107* When the natural advantages of a region for the production of a particular good decline, firms producing the good are bound to move elsewhere.

Acquired advantages of being located in a particular region may be important to a firm's production costs. d

108* From the law of diminishing returns we can tell how an entrepreneur will combine his factors of production.

Relative costs of factors of production will help to decide how an entrepreneur will combine his factors of production. d

5 SUPPLY: DECIDING ON THE MOST PROFITABLE OUTPUT

109 The opportunity cost of a factor of production is:
  a. what it is earning in its present use
  b. what it can earn in the long period
  c. what it can earn in some other use
  d. what has to be paid to retain it in its present use

The following information and choices refer to questions 110 to 112. Mr Smith is a decorator working on his own account. He could earn £24 per week as a painter working for somebody else. Ignore interest charges on his capital. His outgoings and receipts are:

Equipment £200, depreciating at	£1 per week
Insurance against accidents	£1 per week
Necessary minimum compensation for uncertainty	£2 per week
Wallpaper, paint, travelling expenses	£20 per week
Receipts from work done	£50 per week

  a. £41   *b.* £28
  c. £15   *d.* £2

110 What is his 'total' profit per week?

111 What is his 'normal' profit per week?

112 What is his 'abnormal' profit per week?

113 If average cost is falling, marginal cost must be:
  a. falling
  b. rising
  c. less than average cost
  d. more than average cost but falling

114 Which one of the following would be a variable cost to a firm?

a. mortgage repayment on the factory

b. depreciation of machines owing to age

c. debenture interest

d. payments for raw materials

115 The cost accountant of Kitchenware Ltd, which manufactures sink units under conditions of perfect competition, informs the managing director that while receipts from sales are covering the cost of raw materials and wages, they are not sufficient to cover the cost of producing the present output when depreciation of the factory building and plant is taken into account. Which one of the following decisions is the managing director likely to take?

a. call an extraordinary meeting of the shareholders and recommend that the company goes into liquidation

b. give workers a week's notice, and cease producing at the end of that period until prospects seem better

c. cut back production and review the situation in two months' time

d. continue to produce the current output but review the situation in two months' time

The following diagrams and choices refer to questions 116 to 118. The diagrams show: (i) demand and supply in a perfectly competitive industry; (ii) the cost curves of an individual firm in that industry:

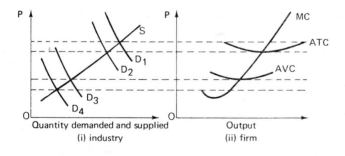

a. D_1 *b.* D_2 *c.* D_3 *d.* D_4

116   What conditions of demand as depicted by the different demand curves will enable the firm to make abnormal profits?

117   Which demand curve will just enable the firm to produce in the long period?

118   Which demand curve represents the minimum demand which will enable the firm to produce in the short period?

119   A firm is said to be producing its optimum size output if:
   a. price equals average cost
   b. price equals marginal cost
   c. average total cost is a minimum
   d. average variable cost is a minimum

120   If a firm operates under conditions of perfect competition, an increase in its output:
   a. will have no effect on price or on total revenue
   b. reduce price, but increase total revenue
   c. have no effect on price, but increase total revenue
   d. reduce both price and total revenue

121   Which of the following conditions are essential for a firm to be producing under perfect competition?
   I The firm sees the market price as given.
   II Other firms can enter the industry easily.
   III A change in consumer's demand has a considerable influence on the price of the commodity.
   IV Changes in the industry's supply have little effect on the price of the commodity.
   V The commodity produced by firms in the industry is identical.
   a. III only   *b.* I, IV, V
   c. I, II, III, IV, V   *d.* I, II, V

The following information about a firm refers to questions 122 to 128.

Output (units)	0	1	2	3	4	5	6	7	8	9
Total revenue (£)	—	10	20	30	40	50	60	70	80	90
Total cost (£)	20	28	30	34	36	37	38	42	50	64

The following choices refer to questions 122 to 125.

   a. £6   *b.* £10
   c. £20   *d.* £30

122 What is the price of the product per unit?

123 What are the firm's fixed costs?

124 What are the firm's profits at its equilibrium output?

125 What is the minimum price at which the firm will produce in the long period?

The following choices refer to questions 126 to 128.

   a. 5 units   *b.* 6 units
   c. 7 units   *d.* 8 units

126 What is the firm's equilibrium output?

127 What is its minimum short period output?

128 What is the optimum size of the firm?

The following diagram refers to questions 129 to 136. It shows the costs and prices facing a profit-maximising firm which is producing under conditions of perfect competition:

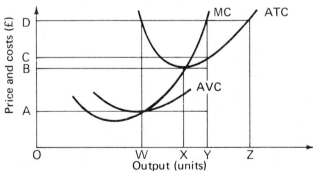

The following choices apply to questions 129 to 133.

   a. OA   *b.* OB
   c. OC   *d.* OD

129   What will be the price when marginal revenue is OD?

130   What will be the lowest price at which the firm can produce in the long period?

131   Below what price will the firm stop producing even in the short period?

132   What price will give it a profit margin of OY × DC?

133   What is the price at which the firm is just making normal profits?

The following choices apply to questions 134 to 136.

   a. OW   *b.* OX
   c. OY   *d.* OZ

134   What output will it produce at a price of OD?

135   What is its minimum short period output?

136   What is the optimum size of the firm?

137   Assume a firm wishes to maximise its profits. Which of the following conditions will, at any given price, ensure an output, n, which will achieve this?

  I Average cost is at a minimum.
  II Price = marginal cost.
  III Marginal revenue = marginal cost.
  IV Average variable cost is at a minimum.
  V Price is at least equal to minimum average variable cost.
  VI At $n-1$ units of output, marginal cost is less than marginal revenue; at $n+1$ units of output, marginal cost is greater than marginal revenue.

   a. I only   *b.* II and V
   c. III, V and VI   *d.* II and IV

138 The following conditions refer to the costs of a firm which is part of a perfectly competitive industry.

I Average total cost is at a minimum.
II Price equals average total cost.
III Price is at least equal to average variable costs.
IV Marginal cost equals marginal revenue.
V Price equals marginal revenue.

Which of the above are the minimum conditions necessary to indicate that the industry is in equilibrium?

a. I, II, III, IV, V   b. I, II
c. I, II, III   d. I, II, III, V

139 A firm obtains the following prices for its goods at different levels of output:

Output (units)	Price (£)
20	26
21	25
22	24
23	23

What is its marginal revenue when it increases output from 21 to 22 units?

a. £4   b. £3
c. £2   d. £1

140 A monopolist, producing under conditions of increasing costs, seeks to maximise his profits. He will produce the output where:

a. total receipts are at a maximum
b. he obtains the highest possible price for his product
c. price equals marginal cost
d. the addition to his total revenue just equals the addition to his total costs

141   The following demand schedule faces a monopolist owner of a spring of water with health properties:

Price (pence per bottle)	Bottles demanded (thousands)
50	90
40	160
30	200
20	250

Assuming that he has no marginal costs, what price per bottle would it be most profitable for him to charge?

a. 50p   *b.* 40p
c. 30p   *d.* 20p

The following diagram, which shows the demand curve and cost curves facing a monopolist, refers to questions 142 to 147.

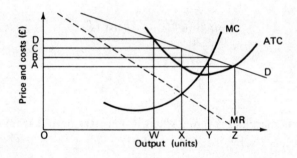

The following choices refer to questions 142 to 145.

a. OA   *b.* OB
c. OC   *d.* OD

142   What is the highest possible price the monopolist could charge and still 'break even'?

143   What is the lowest possible price the monopolist could charge and still 'break even', without there being excess demand?

144   At what price will the monopolist sell his product?

145 What is the average cost per unit at the selling price?

The following choices refer to questions 146 and 147.

   a. OW   *b.* OX
   c. OY   *d.* OZ

146 What is the monopolist's equilibrium output? *b*

147 What is the maximum output he could produce and still cover his costs? *d*

148 A monopolist will always find it profitable to reduce output if:

   a. demand for his product is inelastic at the current price   *a*
   b. demand for his product is elastic at the current price
   c. at the current output, marginal revenue exceeds marginal cost
   d. at the current output, average cost exceeds marginal revenue

149 The diagram shows the demand (average revenue) and marginal revenue curves facing a monopolist.

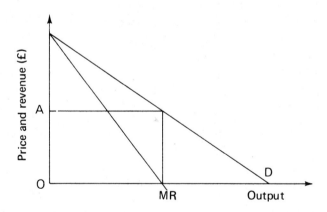

Which of the following statements is true?

  I At price OA, total revenue is at a maximum.
  II The monopolist will only produce at a price of OA if his marginal costs are zero.

III Where he has marginal costs, the monopolist will charge a higher price than OA.

IV Where he has marginal costs, the monopolist will produce at a price where demand is elastic.

    a. I and II   *b.* II only

    c. I, II and III   *d.* I, II, III and IV

150 At a local football cup-tie the gates have been closed and only ticket-holders are being allowed in. A 'spiv' outside finds he is the only person with tickets. Each ticket cost him £1. If he wishes to maximise his profit he should charge a price per ticket which

    a. just ensures that each ticket is sold

    b. maximises his total receipts

    c. yields the greatest profit per ticket sold

    d. ensures that he disposes of all his tickets as quickly as possible

The following information and choices refer to questions 151 to 153. A local newspaper has 60 units of advertising space to sell. Its representative reports the following results of his enquiries:

    40 firms would be willing to pay £6 per unit of space

    50 firms would be willing to pay £5 per unit of space

    60 firms would be willing to pay £4 per unit of space

    70 firms would be willing to pay £3 per unit of space

Assume that there is no way in which advertisers can discover what others have paid and that the costs of setting up the type are so small that they can be ignored.

    a. £360   *b.* £330

    c. £250   *d.* £240

151 What will the newspaper's receipts be if it sells at a single price just sufficient to dispose of the 60 units?

152 What will the newspaper's receipts be if it sells at a single price with the aim of maximising its profits?

153 What will the newspaper's receipts be if it fixes different prices in units of £1 charging each advertiser the price which the representative considers each is willing to pay?

First statement

154* The sole objective of a firm is always to maximise short-term profits.

Second statement

A firm's profit-maximising output is that where marginal revenue equals marginal cost.

6 THE SUPPLY CURVE OF THE INDUSTRY

The following information refers to questions 155 and 156. An industry producing X is composed of 50 firms, whose marginal costs (in £) are as follows:

Output of units	5 firms like A	10 firms like B	15 firms like C	20 firms like D
1	2	4	6	8
2	4	6	8	10
3	6	8	10	12
4	8	10	12	14
5	10	12	14	16
6	12	14	16	18
7	14	16	18	20

The following choices refer to questions 155 and 156.

   a. 200 units   *b.* 150 units
   c. 100 units   *d.* 50 units

155 What quantity is supplied when the market price of X is £6 per unit?

156 What quantity is supplied when the market price of X is £12 per unit?

The following choices refer to questions 157 and 158.

   a. 15   *b.* 30
   c. 45   *d.* 50

157 How many firms comprise the 'industry' at a price of £4?

158 If the price rises to £6, how many firms comprise the industry?

The following diagrams and choices refer to questions 159 to 162. The diagram shows the cost curve of firms in a perfectly competitive industry and the supply curve has been 'smoothed'. D_1, D_2, etc. represent different conditions of demand.

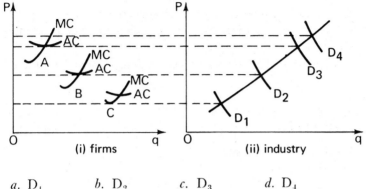

a. D_1 b. D_2 c. D_3 d. D_4

159 What will be the conditions of demand when all firms in the industry are making abnormal profits?

160 What will be the conditions of demand when all firms are forced out of the industry?

161 What will be the conditions of demand when firms like B are marginal?

162 What will be the conditions of demand when it becomes profitable for firms like A to enter the industry?

163 I All firms are producing where price = marginal cost.
II All firms are producing where they are making no abnormal profits.
III All firms are producing where price = minimum average total cost.
IV All firms are producing where total revenue = total cost.

Which of the above conditions are true when a perfectly competitive industry is in equilibrium in the long period:

a. I, III only   b. II only
c. I, II, III, IV   d. I and II only

164 The supply of the industry at any price consists of:

   a. the output of those firms which are just making normal profit
   b. the equilibrium output of all firms producing
   c. the output of all firms which are producing at their optimum size
   d. the output of all firms which are making abnormal profits

165 Under conditions of imperfect competition, profits are maximised when:

   I Price equals marginal cost.
   II Price equals average cost.
   III Marginal cost equals marginal revenue.
   IV Marginal cost is greater than marginal revenue.

Which of these statements is true?

   a. III only   *b.* II and IV
   c. I only   *d.* I and IV

166 Which one of the following conditions applies to monopolistic competition but not to monopoly?

   a. the firm faces a downward-sloping demand curve
   b. free entry to the industry
   c. marginal revenue is less than price
   d. the firm produces where marginal cost equals marginal revenue

167 A profit-maximising firm may incur advertising costs in order to:

   a. make the demand for its products more elastic
   b. reduce the amount of corporation tax it pays
   c. attract other firms into the industry
   d. convince people that its product is different from that of possible competitors

The following table and choices refer to questions 168 and 169.

Price (£) per unit	Quantity supplied (units) per week
5	20
6	28
7	49

a. 2   b. 3
c. 4   d. 5

168 Which one of the above is the elasticity of supply when price rises from £5 to £6?

169 Which one of the above is the elasticity of supply when price falls from £7 to £6?

170

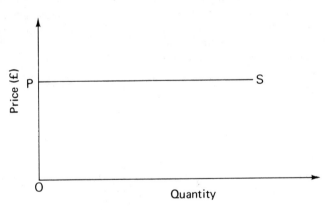

The above supply curve shows:

a. varying quantities of X will be put on the market as price rises or falls
b. no X will be supplied whatever the price
c. the same quantity of X will be put on the market at price OP
d. there is no definite limit to the amount of X which will be supplied at price OP

171 There is a given decrease in demand for commodity X. The greater the elasticity of supply of X:

   a. the greater will be the fall in price and the smaller will be the fall in the quantity of X sold

   b. the greater will be the fall in price and the greater the fall in the quantity of X sold

   c. the smaller will be the fall in price and the smaller will be the fall in the quantity of X sold

   d. the smaller will be the fall in price and the greater will be the fall in the quantity of X sold

First statement	*Second statement*
172* In both monopoly and monopolistic competition, marginal revenue is less than price at any given output.	Producers under monopoly and monopolistic competition face a downward-sloping demand curve for their products.
173* Where a firm is part of an industry in which conditions of monopolistic competition prevail, it will not make any abnormal profit in the long period.	There is free entry of firms to the industry under conditions of monopolistic competition.

7 THE DETERMINATION OF FACTOR PRICES

174 Which one of the following is a derived demand as opposed to a direct demand by consumers?

  a. an author's typewriter
  b. a family holiday in Spain
  c. flower bulbs for the garden of a private house
  d. a child's tricycle

175 The revenue-productivity of a factor is determined by:

  a. the price at which the product sells
  b. the productivity of the factor
  c. the price at which the product sells and the productivity of the factor
  d. the reward offered to the factor

176 In the diagram, the curve MRP represents the base position. Which one of the following changes is likely to move the curve to MRP_1?

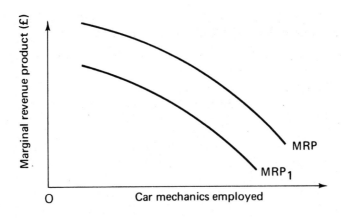

   a. greater productivity by car mechanics
   b. people spending more of their income on motoring
   c. a considerable fall in the price of cars
   d. a substantial rise in the tax on petrol

177 A firm is one of many in a perfectly competitive industry making felt toys. Raw material and other variable costs are relatively so small that they can be ignored. The productivity of its employees varies according to the number employed because capital equipment is fixed in supply:

Number of employees	Total output of toys per week
6	350
7	378
8	402
9	424
10	442

When employee's wages are £22 per week, the firm employs 9 workers. If employees' wages rose to £24 per week, the firm would be most likely to:

   a. increase its output of toys to 442 per week
   b. dismiss 1 employee
   c. dismiss 2 employees
   d. scrap its least efficient machine

178 It can be safely said that any profit maximising employer will hire units of a variable factor up to the point where:

   a. its marginal revenue product equals its marginal cost
   b. diminishing returns operate
   c. its marginal revenue product becomes zero
   d. its marginal revenue product equals the wage rate

The following diagram refers to questions 179 to 183. It illustrates the MRP of television mechanics when added to fixed factors in the short period. MRP_1 represents a lower price charged for repairs than MRP_2, and MRP_2 a lower price than MRP_3.

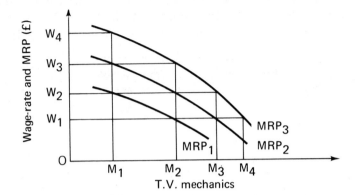

The following choices refer to questions 179 and 180.

   a. M_1 *b.* M_2 *c.* M_3 *d.* M_4

179 At the lower price of repairs (MRP_1), how many mechanics will be employed at a wage rate of OW_1?

180 At the highest price of repairs (MRP_3), how many mechanics will be employed at a wage rate of OW_2?

The following choices refer to questions 181 and 182.

   a. OW_1 *b.* OW_2 *c.* OW_3 *d.* OW_4

181 If there are OM_2 mechanics what, at the lowest price of repairs, can be the maximum wage rate if they are all to be fully employed?

182 If there are OM_3 mechanics what, at the highest price of repairs, can be the maximum wage rate if they are all to be fully employed.

183 If the MRP_2 curve represents the base position, which one of the following changes would move the curve towards MRP_1?

   a. a greatly increased demand for secondhand television sets
   b. greater productivity by television mechanics
   c. higher charges for television repairs
   d. people spending more of their income on motoring and home decoration and less on television

The following tables and choices refer to questions 184 and 185. The table shows the relationship between the total output of wheat on a given plot of land and the number of men employed:

Men employed	Total output of wheat (tons per year)
3	66
4	81
5	90
6	96

a. 3   b. 4
c. 5   d. 6

184 If other costs are so small that they can be ignored and wheat sells at £50 a ton, how many men would be employed at a yearly salary of £720?

185 How many will be employed if the yearly salary fell to £400?

186 The developer of a city centre site finds that as he builds upwards costs per unit of additional accommodation increase. As a result, given additions of capital increase the value of the building as follows:

Capital (£ th.)	Total value of building (£ th.)
10	60
20	75
30	87
40	98
50	106

How much capital (in £ th.) will he spend in building?

a. 20   b. 30
c. 40   d. 50

187 If a firm employs land up to the point where its marginal revenue product is zero, it means that:

a. land is free
b. factors which are combined with the land have no price
c. land is absolutely inelastic in supply
d. it is expensive to hire labour

188 Which one of the following changes, other things being equal, is likely to cause the wage rate of bricklayers to rise:

    a. a decrease in the demand for houses
    b. a depression in the building industry in Eire
    c. a decrease in the productivity of bricklayers
    d. a reduction in the number of bricklayers entering the industry

The following table and choices refer to questions 189 and 190. Labour represents a variable factor used in conjunction with fixed quantities of machines, land and capital:

Number of men employed	Output per week	Price per unit received by a monopolist producer
5	16	23
6	20	22
7	23	21
8	25	20
9	27	19

    a. 6   *b.* 7
    c. 8   *d.* 9

189 How many men will be employed if the wage-rate is £42 per week?

190 How many men will be employed if the wage-rate is £16 per week?

191 Where the wage-rate of labour is less than the marginal cost of labour, a firm hiring such labour will be:

    a. selling its product in a perfectly competitive market
    b. selling its product under conditions of imperfect competition
    c. buying labour in a perfectly competitive market
    d. buying labour under conditions of imperfect competition

First statement	*Second statement*
192* Under perfect competition, a factor will be demanded up to the point where its MRP equals its price.	*In practice* the reward paid to a factor depends entirely upon its productivity and the price of the product it makes.

8   LABOUR AND WAGES

The following table refers to questions 193 to 196.

Year	Index of retail prices	Total money wages (£)	Total number employed	Average weekly hours worked
a	50	10,000	100	50
b	75	18,000	100	50
c	100	26,000	130	40
d	150	36,000	140	30

193   In which year were average money wages per worker the highest?

194   In which year were total real wages the highest?

195   In which year were average real wages per worker the highest?

196   In which year were average real wages per man hour the highest?

197   Which one of the following will lead to a rise in the demand for docker's labour in the UK?

a. the adoption of tariff protection by the UK
b. a reduction in the cost of air freight
c. an increase in the price of labour-saving cranes and containers
d. a rise in dockers' wage-rates

198

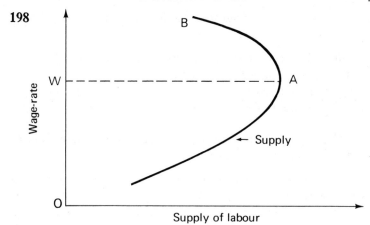

Supply of labour

The backward sloping curve AB is explained by the fact that when the wage-rate rises above OW:

    a. workers prefer to substitute work for leisure

    b. workers' income has increased to the point at which, at present relative prices, other goods are inferior to leisure

    c. immigration is more strictly controlled

    d. unemployment develops

199 I Labour as a whole in a country having immigration restrictions.

    II Labour in a particular occupation.

    III Labour of an individual worker.

A backward sloping long-run supply curve is a realistic possibility for:

    a. I only   *b.* I, II, III

    c. III   *d.* I and III

200 Which of the following changes would be likely to produce an increase in electricians' wages?

    a. a major depression in the construction industry

    b. an increase in the number of apprentices qualifying as electricians

    c. an increase in the prices of electricity and of electrical appliances

    d. a large reduction in the price of electricity

201 The size of the labour force of the UK is influenced directly by all the following *except*:

   a. the minimum school-leaving age
   b. the age-distribution of the population
   c. immigration policy
   d. An increase in VAT

202 The main cause of differences in wages of women in retailing in different parts of the country is:

   a. demand for goods sold in retail shops is lower in the lower paid districts
   b. women are better organised in trade unions in the high-wage areas
   c. female labour does not move easily from the lower to the higher paid districts
   d. in the lower paid districts a higher proportion of women prefer shop to other forms of work

203 If solicitors receive higher salaries than schoolteachers it is mainly because:

   a. they work longer hours than schoolteachers
   b. teaching is more pleasant work
   c. there is a higher proportion of schoolteachers than solicitors
   d. people with solicitor's training are relatively more scarce than schoolteachers

204 In Year 1 the wage-rate in an industry is determined by competitive market forces at 50p an hour. The government considers this too low and, without any other adjustment of policy, fixes a minimum rate of 80p an hour. The result will be:

   a. all workers employed in the industry will obtain the higher rate of 80p
   b. no workers will obtain the higher rate because unemployment will occur
   c. some workers will obtain the higher rate and some will be unemployed
   d. no workers will be employed at the higher wage rate

Questions 205 to 207 are based on the following information. Country X imports two-thirds of her foodstuffs from abroad. There are no import duties or other trade restrictions. International transport developments lead to a considerable fall in the cost of transporting foodstuffs.

205 What will be the likely effect on the price of home-produced foodstuffs and the quantity sold?

    a. price will increase, quantity sold will increase
    b. price will increase, quantity sold will decrease
    c. price will decrease, quantity sold will decrease
    d. price will decrease, quantity sold will increase

206 Which of the following will be the effect on the conditions of employment of agricultural labourers in country X assuming that there is no change in their productivity?

    a. wages can fall and the same number of workers be employed
    b. wages can rise with the same number of workers being employed
    c. both wages and the number employed can rise
    d. both wages and the number employed can remain unchanged

207 Which of the following changes in the distribution of real income will result from the change?

I The real income of agricultural labourers will fall relative to people in X generally.
II The real income of people generally in X will rise.
III Wage-earners with large families will gain relatively in real income compared with rich people with small families.

    a. I only   *b.* I and III
    c. I, II and III   *d.* II and III

208 In conditions of full employment, a trade union is likely to be successful in obtaining a wage increase when:

    a. the demand for the product made by the labour is elastic
    b. the supply of labour-saving equipment is elastic
    c. labour costs form a very small proportion of total costs
    d. a large part of the product made by the labour is sold on foreign markets

209 A profit-maximising monopolist seller of his product will employ labour up to the point where:

   a. the marginal physical product of labour multiplied by the price of the product equals the wage-rate

   b. the marginal physical product of labour multiplied by the price of the product equals the marginal cost of labour

   c. the marginal physical product of labour multiplied by the marginal revenue from the sale of the product equals the wage-rate

   d. the wage-rate equals the price of the product

	First statement	*Second statement*
210*	The demand for power-station electricians is likely to be inelastic.	Except in the very long period, the demand for electricity tends to be inelastic.

9 CAPITAL AND INTEREST

211 The difference between capital and income is:

a. capital is a stock of wealth, whereas income is a flow of wealth over a period of time

b. capital can be used over and over again whereas income cannot

c. capital is wealth whereas income refers to a person's standard of living

d. capital is wealth that cannot be used up, whereas income is wealth that is consumed

The following information and choices refer to questions 212 and 213. A man prepares the following statement for his accountant:

Yearly salary	£3,100
Value of shares held in companies	2,200
Deposits in building society	900
Interest on shares and deposits	250
Family allowances	50

a. £3,100   b. £3,200
c. £3,300   d. £3,400

212 What is his yearly income?

213 What is his capital?

214 Which one of the following would be included in a calculation of national capital?

a. Premium Bonds

b. pictures in the National Portrait Gallery

c. funds held in the National Savings Bank

d. Treasury bills held by the Commercial banks

215 The main reason why capital-using methods of production have not been introduced more by the under-developed countries is:

    a. the greater productivity of capital-using methods is not appreciated

    b. the introduction of capital-using methods would lead to widespread unemployment

    c. the allocation of factors to producing them is determined by the central government instead of through a price system

    d. countries cannot afford the sacrifice of present consumption which more rapid accumulation of capital would entail

The following choices refer to questions 216 and 217.

    a. a carpet worth £10

    b. a £10 note

    c. £10 in the National Savings Bank

    d. £10 in a building society deposit

216 Which one of the above is the most liquid asset?

217 Which one of the above is the least liquid asset?

218 Which one of the following statements is true?

    a. raising the rate of interest will always cause people to save more

    b. consumers who buy goods on hire purchase at a high rate of interest show that they have a high rate of 'time-preference'

    c. the rate of interest which has to be paid to borrow funds is determined solely by the demand for and supply of such funds

    d. the rate of interest charged by a commercial bank for an overdraft is determined solely by the amount of funds it has to lend

219 The 'liquidity' of an asset refers to how easily it can be:

    a. withdrawn from where it has been deposited

    b. exchanged for other assets

    c. divided into smaller units

    d. stored

220 'Liquidity preference' is best indicated by:
 a. buying government stock rather than household goods
 b. buying low-yielding rather than high-yielding stock
 c. holding money rather than other assets
 d. asking to be paid in cash rather than by cheque

221 Which one of the following represents the percentage long-term rate of interest if the price on the Stock Exchange of £100 nominal undated 2½ per cent Consols is £40?
 a. $6\frac{1}{4}$ *b.* 7
 c. $8\frac{1}{2}$ *d.* 9

222 If the long-term rate of interest falls from 10 to 7 per cent, the price at which undated 3½ per cent War Loan sells on the Stock Exchange will:
 a. fall from £50 to £35
 b. rise from £35 to £50
 c. stay unchanged at £100
 d. fall from £100 to £70

223 In an effort to control inflation, the government unexpectedly relies heavily on monetary policy and there is a significant rise in the long-term rate of interest. Those most adversely affected by this will be the holders of:
 a. equities
 b. Treasury bills
 c. long-term bonds
 d. building society deposits

224 People will tend to demand money if they think:
 a. taxation will be increased
 b. the government will increase the supply of money
 c. the price of bonds will rise
 d. the price of bonds will fall

225 People will tend to move out of money into bonds if they think:
 a. the rate of interest is going to fall
 b. the rate of interest is going to rise
 c. the rate of interest is not going to change
 d. the price of real goods will fall

First statement	*Second statement*
226* Income is a flow of wealth over time.	Capital is a stock of wealth existing at a given moment of time.

10 LAND AND RENT

227 The main reason why more rent has to be paid for office space in the high blocks in the centre of London than in the three storey buildings in a provincial town is:

    a. high office blocks cost more to build

    b. the land on which London office blocks are built costs more

    c. office blocks are owned by just a few companies who combine together to charge high rents

    d. in London there is a larger number of office users willing to pay high prices who compete for the limited space

228 Economic rent is:

    a. the difference between a factor's actual and transfer earnings

    b. what a factor earns in the short period

    c. the transfer earnings of a factor in the short period

    d. the earnings of a factor whose supply is not perfectly elastic

The following information and choices refer to questions 229 and 230. A small strip of land, 3 metres wide, runs between two houses owned by A and B. The land is owned by a third person C. A is keen on gardening whereas B is not; A therefore rents the land from C at £5 per year.

Just at the time A's lease expires, B acquires a car and offers C £20 per year for the land in order to build a garage. This offer is accepted:

    a. £5   *b.* £10   *c.* £15   *d.* £20

229 What was the economic rent per year on the plot before B bought his car?

230 What was the economic rent per year on the plot after B bought his car?

231 Assuming the supply of coffee-growing land is fixed, a 50 per cent *ad valorem* tax on coffee-growing land will result in:

    a. a 50 per cent increase in the rent paid by coffee-growers

    b. an increase in the price of coffee

    c. a 50 per cent decrease in the rent received (net) by owners of the land on which coffee is grown

    d. none of the above

232 Which one of the following statements is *false?*

    a. the earnings of capital equipment whose supply cannot be increased is rent

    b. if a factor is absolutely fixed in supply, its return will depend entirely upon what the product it makes sells for

    c. the economic rent earned by a factor is the difference between its earnings and its opportunity cost

    d. economic rent cannot be earned by a factor in conditions of perfect competition

233 Economic rent will *not* be earned by a factor if:

    a. the demand for it is perfectly elastic

    b. the supply of it is perfectly elastic

    c. the demand for it is perfectly inelastic

    d. it has no alternative uses

234 A footballer could earn £30 per week as a clerk, £35 per week as a salesman, and £40 per week as a surveyor. At present, however, he is paid £100 per week by his club. His economic rent is therefore:

    a. £70   *b.* £65

    c. £60   *d.* £55

The following diagram and choices refer to questions 235 and 236.

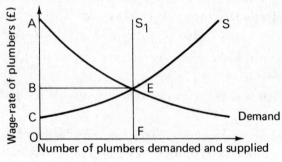

    a. ABE   *b.* BCE

    c. BOFE   *d.* COFE

235 If the supply curve for plumbers is S, what is the economic rent earned by plumbers as a whole?   *b*

236 Supposing that the supply curve for plumbers was S_1, what would be the economic rent earned by plumbers?   *c*

237 'Quasi-rent' refers to the earnings of:

    a. land held on short lease
    b. land in the long period
    c. any durable factor in the long period
    d. any factor of production in the short period when the supply is fixed   *d*

First statement	*Second statement*	
238* When the supply of a factor is absolutely inelastic, the whole of the return to it is economic rent.	The return to a factor fixed in supply will depend entirely upon the price at which the product it makes sells.	*b*
239* Given an unchanged demand for offices in the City of London, a rise in the cost of building offices will lead to higher rents being charged.	Developers will have to offer a lower price for land upon which to build offices in the City.	*d*

11   ENTREPRENEURSHIP AND PROFIT

240   Which one of the following risks could *not* be insured against?

  a. heavy rain on the day of a church fete
  b. twins being born to your wife
  c. the failure of a West End play
  d. the theft of your colour television set

241   An economist makes the following deductions from the revenue of a tobacconist in calculating his profits for the year:

  a. shop-girl's wages
  b. cost of stock sold
  c. rent of shop
  d. how much the tobacconist could earn in his best alternative occupation

Which one of the above would *not* be included by the accountant when calculating profit?

The following information and choices refer to questions 242 to 246. A decorator, working on his own account, could earn £24 per week if employed by a firm. When he is self-employed, his weekly costs and receipts (ignoring interest charges or allowances for capital employed) are:

Van – original cost £500, depreciating at £2 per week

Tax and insurance on van	£2
Petrol and oil for running van	£2
Shed for equipment	£2
Paint and paper	£10
Necessary minimum compensation for uncertainty	£2
Receipts for work done	£56

  a. £2 per week   b. £12 per week
  c. £38 per week   d. £44 per week

242   What is his total profit in an accounting sense?

243 What would be his normal profit as estimated by an economist?

244 What is his abnormal profit?

245 What are the minimum receipts he must take each week if he is to remain working on his own account in the short period, assuming that he has savings upon which he can live?

246 What are the minimum receipts he must take each week if he is to remain working on his own account in the long period?

247 Which one of the following firms would require the highest rate of normal profit?

   a. a newsagent
   b. a company letting shop premises in the High Street
   c. a firm drilling for oil in the North Sea
   d. a garage selling petrol

248 Which one of the following statements is *false?*

   a. profit can be both a cost and a residual reward
   b. under perfect competition, normal profit disappears in the long period
   c. normal profit is necessary to induce entrepreneurs to accept the risks of uncertainty
   d. since abnormal profit is a residual reward it plays no part in the operation of the private enterprise economy

249 Which one of the following statements is correct for a fully competitive private enterprise economy?

   a. one of the main functions of profits is to give trade unions a measurement of the extent to which labour is being exploited
   b. high profits in an industry indicate to the government that wages are too low in that industry
   c. one of the functions of profits is to attract new entrants into an industry so that prices will be forced down to the point where only normal profit is made
   d. losses incurred by certain industries indicate that the private enterprise system is not working effectively

First statement	*Second statement*
250* Under perfect competition, abnormal profit is the reward for uncertainty-bearing.	Under perfect competition, normal profit disappears in the long period.

12 MONEY AND THE RATE OF INTEREST

251 The essential attribute which distinguishes money from other assets is:

   a. general acceptability

   b. can be stored by banks

   c. made of a durable material

   d. convenient to carry

252 Money has been described as a 'bearer of options'. An alternative way of expressing the same idea is to say that money is:

   a. a most attractive form in which wealth can be held

   b. useful only when it is being spent

   c. only one of a number of things which act as a medium of exchange

   d. a perfectly liquid asset

The following choices refer to questions 253 to 255.

   a. £15   *b.* £30

   c. £45   *d.* £60

A man earns £30 a week, and spends the lot.

253 If he is paid weekly, what is his average holding of money?

254 If he is paid monthly (4 weeks), what is his average holding of money?

255 If his wage is doubled and he is paid weekly, what will now be his average holding of money?

256 People demand money for the precautionary motive because:

   a. the rate of interest is expected to fall

   b. the price of bonds is expected to rise

   c. they need cash for everyday purchases

   d. they wish to provide against unforeseen contingencies

257 Which one of the following will have the major influence on the demand for idle money balances?

    a. the level of income
    b. the desire to provide for a rainy day
    c. the current rate of interest
    d. the frequency with which income is received

258 People will tend to demand money if they expect:

    a. taxation will be increased
    b. the rate of interest will fall
    c. the price of bonds will rise
    d. the rate of interest will rise

259 Other things being equal, which of the following changes will lead to an increased holding of money balances?

I All wages are paid monthly instead of weekly.
II A fall in the level of aggregate incomes.
III People expect that interest rates generally will soon move to a permanently higher level.

    a. I only   *b.* I and III
    c. II and III   *d.* I and II

The following information and choices refer to questions 260 to 262.

(i) the total supply of money in the economy is £6,000 mn.

(ii) the demand for active balances at the current level of income is £2,000 mn.

(iii) the demand for idle balances varies with the rate of interest as follows:

Rate of interest (per cent)	Demand for idle balances (£mn)
9	2,000
8	4,000
7	7,000
6	11,000

    a. 9 per cent   *b.* 8 per cent
    c. 7 per cent   *d.* 6 per cent

260 What will be the current rate of interest in the economy?

261 If the total supply of money had been £13,000 mn what would have been the rate of interest?

262 If, with the total supply of money £13,000 mn, demand for active balances now rises to £6,000 mn, what would be the new rate of interest?

263 Which one of the following would *not* be regarded as 'true' money?

    a. a £10 note
    b. a 50 penny piece
    c. a deposit in a commercial bank upon which cheques can be drawn
    d. a railway season ticket

264 Other things being equal, the rate of interest can be expected to rise if:

    a. the supply of money is increased
    b. entrepreneurs generally expect a falling-off in the profitability of capital equipment
    c. there is an all-round increase in money incomes
    d. the rate of saving increases

265 Other things being equal, which one of the following would be likely to lose by rising prices?

    a. a firm which has recently raised capital by the issue of 10-year debentures
    b. people who have just bought the 10-year debentures
    c. the owner of a Van Gogh painting
    d. a person holding shares in a diamond mine

266 In order to compile the Index of Retail Prices it is necessary to decide on all of the following *except*:

    a. a base year
    b. a basket of goods of the typical family
    c. a 'typical' family
    d. changes in the general level of prices

The following information and choices refer to questions 267 and 268. Assume that: (i) Year I is the base year; (ii) the basket chosen for the Index consists only of two goods, potatoes and meat; (iii) the quantities bought each year are potatoes 10 lbs, meat 4 lbs. Figures represent the price (pence per lb) for three consecutive years:

Year	I	II	III
Potatoes	2	1	2
Meat	20	25	25

a. 100   *b.* 110
c. 120   *d.* 130

267   Which of the above represents the Index in Year II?

268   Which of the above represents the Index in Year III?

First statement	*Second statement*
269* Cheques written on a current account at a bank can be regarded as money.	Money is anything which is generally acceptable in payment of debts.
270* People will demand money if they think that the rate of interest is going to rise.	A rising rate of interest means that the price of bonds is falling.

13 JOINT-STOCK BANKS

271 Cheques have become a medium of exchange because:

   a. they are more convenient for settling debts
   b. they are accepted by most people
   c. they can be written for any amount
   d. they act as receipts

272 A commercial bank can be considered to be following sound banking principles if it could:

   a. repay cash to all its depositors on demand
   b. repay cash to those depositors who are likely to ask for it
   c. repay cash to its depositors as soon as it has realised sufficient of its assets to do so
   d. cash a cheque for any amount at any branch

273 A commercial bank has cash reserves of £8 mn. It creates deposits on the basis of a cash ratio of 8 per cent of total deposits. Which one of the following is the maximum level of total deposits it can maintain?

   a. £8 mn   *b.* £64 mn
   c. £100 mn   *d.* £120 mn

274 A bank creates deposits on the basis of a cash ratio of 8 per cent up to its limit. It then finds that customers start to withdraw cash but do not spend it. If the total amount of cash withdrawn is £20 mn, by how much (in £ mn) do total deposits have to be reduced?

   a. nil   *b.* 20
   c. 125   *d.* 250

275 When borrowers repay a bank loan, the process usually involves:

   a. a reduction in bank assets and bank liabilities

   b. an increase in earning assets and a decrease in liabilities

   c. an increase in earning assets, and a decrease in non-earning assets

   d. a decrease in non-earning assets and a decrease in liabilities

276 Investments are not regarded as 'liquid assets' because:

   a. they cannot be sold quickly on the Stock Exchange

   b. there may be a considerable fall in their capital value if they have to be sold quickly

   c. they yield such a good return that they are best regarded as 'earning assets'

   d. they can be reduced by government open market operations

The following assets of a commercial bank refer to questions 277 to 283.

I advances	II bills discounted
III special deposits	IV money at call
V cash	VI investments

277 The order of these assets as regards profitability is:

   a. I, II, III, IV, VI, V

   b. I, VI, II, III, IV, V

   c. VI, III, I, II, IV, V

   d. I, III, II, IV, VI, V

278 The order of these assets as regards liquidity is:

   a. V, III, IV, II, VI, I

   b. V, II, III, IV, VI, I

   c. V, II, I, VI, III

   d. V, IV, II, VI, I, III

279 Which asset is the 'cushion' between the liquid assets and advances?

   a. II   *b.* III

   c. VI   *d.* IV

280 Which represents a loan to the discount houses?

   a. I   *b.* II   *c.* III   *d.* IV

281 Which is the *chief* earning asset?

   a. I   *b.* II   *c.* III   *d.* VI

282 Which one would be increased directly if the Bank of England bought bonds on the Stock Exchange?

   a. III   *b.* IV   *c.* V   *d.* VI

283 Which one would the authorities like to reduce the most in a 'credit squeeze'?

   a. I   *b.* II   *c.* IV   *d.* VI

284 When bank deposits rise sharply:

   a. people must be saving large sums

   b. interest rates must be increasing

   c. banks generally are making numerous loans

   d. business is slowing down and money flows to the banks

The following information applies to questions 285 to 287. It represents the assets of a commercial bank. All figures are in £ mn.

I	cash	24
II	money at call	22
III	bills discounted	48
IV	special deposits	6
V	investments	50
VI	advances to customers	150

285 What is the cash ratio (per cent)?

   a. 6   *b.* 8   *c.* 10   *d.* 12

286 In view of its distribution of assets, the bank could reduce its holding of:

   a. VI only   *b.* II and III

   c. IV only   *d.* V and VI

287 In view of its distribution of assets, the bank would be likely to increase its holdings of:

   a. I and V   *b.* III only

   c. I and III   *d.* V and VI

First statement	*Second statement*
288* A bank can lend only the money which is deposited with it.	Advances to customers create deposits.

14 THE BANK OF ENGLAND

289 The Bank of England performs all the following *except*:

   a. issuing notes

   b. accepting deposits from commercial banks

   c. lending to the commercial banks when they are short of cash

   d. advancing money to the government

The following information refers to questions 290 to 293.
Assume:

   (i) a clearing bank's assets consist of cash and advances only;

  (ii) customers are wanting advances;

 (iii) the same cash ratio is maintained;

 (iv) all securities are bought by customers of the bank;

  (v) the following is the bank's asset structure.

	£mn
Cash	200
Advances	1,800
Total deposits	2,000

The following choices refer to questions 290 and 291.

   a. £180 mn   *b.* £220 mn

   c. £280 mn   *d.* £380 mn

290 What cash will be held by the bank if the Bank of England sells £20 mn of government securities on the Stock Exchange?

291 By how much will its advances change as a result of this sale?
The following choices refer to questions 292 and 293.

   a. £160 mn   *b.* £240 mn

   c. £360 mn   *d.* £480 mn

292 What cash will be held by the bank if, on the original information, the Bank of England buys £40 mn of government securities on the Stock Exchange?

293 By how much will advances change as a result of this purchase?

294 Which of the following interest rates is *most* closely under the day-to-day control of the monetary authorities?

    a. bank overdraft rate

    b. discount rate on Treasury Bills

    c. bank 'call money' rate

    d. building society deposit rate?

295 Which of the following institutions is *not* directly concerned with dealings in Treasury Bills?

    a. discount houses

    b. the Bank of England

    c. the Stock Exchange

    d. the commercial banks

296 Which one of the following institutions will be affected most directly by an increase in Treasury Bills offered at the weekly tender?

    a. building societies

    b. discount houses

    c. acceptance houses

    d. savings banks

297 Other things being equal, an increase in Treasury Bills offered at the weekly tender will result in:

    a. a flow of short-term funds out of the UK

    b. a fall in the rate charged on overdrafts

    c. a rise in the price at which Treasury Bills are sold

    d. a rise in the rate at which Treasury Bills are discounted

298 Which of the following measures will directly affect the yield on government bonds?

    a. open market operations

    b. a change in the liquidity ratio

    c. directives

    d. special deposits

299 Which of the following is most likely to lead to an increase in bank deposits?

    a. a reduction in the Fiduciary Issue

    b. a reduction in Treasury Bills offered at the weekly tender *c.* a reduction in special deposits

d. an increase in the liquidity ratio

300 The following are possible actions which could be taken by the Bank of England:

I Buy securities on the open market.

II Lower the minimum liquidity ratio.

III Call for special deposits.

IV Increase funding of the National Debt.

Which of the above actions would be consistent with a 'tight money' policy?

a. I, III and IV   *b.* III and IV

c. I and III   *d.* I and IV

301 When the Bank of England wishes to restrict the power of the commercial banks to create credit it could:

a. lower the minimum liquidity ratio

b. call for special deposits

c. purchase securities on the open market

d. borrow through Treasury Bills rather than long-term bonds

302 Which of the following policies would be most appropriate for the Bank of England to follow if it wished to make it more difficult for the commercial banks to grant loans?

a. carry out open market operations by buying long-term stock

b. raise the percentage of special deposits required

c. increase the maximum period of repayment on hire purchase agreements

d. reduce the percentage deposit required on hire purchase transactions

303 Which one of the following would be consistent with an expansionary monetary policy?

a. an increase in the liquidity ratio

b. an increase in the percentage deposit required on hire purchase commitments

c. an extension of the maximum period of repayment of hire purchase commitments

d. a sale of securities on the open market

First statement	Second statement
304* A release by the Bank of England of special deposits would be consistent with an expansionary monetary policy.	Special deposits are included as part of a bank's eligible reserve assets.

15 GOVERNMENT FINANCE

The following choices refer to questions 305 to 308.

a. 5 per cent   *b.* 10 per cent
c. 20 per cent   *d.* 40 per cent

305 Which of the above represents the approximate percentage of the Gross National Product of the UK which in 1976 was taken by central and local government taxation?

306 Which of the above represents the approximate percentage of the Gross National Product of the UK which in 1976 was spent by local authorities?

307 Which of the above represents the approximate percentage of the Gross National Product of the UK which in 1976 was spent on defence?

308 Which of the above represents the approximate percentage of the Gross National Product of the UK which in 1976 was spent on the social services (including education)?

309 Which one of the following would *not* be included in the National Debt?

a. long-term government bonds
b. National Savings Certificates
c. local authority bonds
d. Premium Bonds

310 A budget is best described as:

a. a list of expenditure made the previous year
b. an estimate of expected income and a plan for expenditure
c. a means of raising money for necessary expenditure
d. a plan for purchasing the best quality goods at the lowest prices

311 Taxes which may be shifted from the person upon whom they are originally imposed to another person are:

    a. specific taxes
    b. double taxes
    c. proportional taxes
    d. indirect taxes

The different taxes which follow refer to questions 312 to 314.

    I capital gains tax   II income tax
  III value-added-tax   IV capital transfer tax
    V corporation tax   VI petrol duty

312 Which of the above is a tax on capital?

    a. I, II and IV   *b.* I only
    c. I and IV   *d.* IV and V

313 Which of the above is an indirect tax?

    a. I, III and VI   *b.* III and VI
    c. V and VI   *d.* III, V and VI

314 Which of the above is a tax on income or on the profits of companies?

    a. I, II and VI   *b.* II only
    c. II and IV   *d.* II and V

315 Where in the production of a good there are social benefits above the private benefits derived directly by the consumers, the government may:

    a. grant a subsidy towards the production of the good
    b. impose a specific tax on the good
    c. impose an *ad valorem* tax on the good
    d. control the maximum price at which the good can be sold

316 A tax will have an automatic stabilising effect on the economy if its yield:

    a. increases with a fall in income
    b. decreases with a rise in income
    c. decreases with a decrease in income
    d. remains constant as income rises

317 The income tax system of country X exempts the first £1,000 of income from tax and has a flat rate of tax on the remainder of 30 per cent. Which one of the following statements is true?

a. people with large incomes pay the same average rate of tax as people with small incomes

b. people with large incomes pay the same marginal rate of tax as people with small incomes

c. people with small incomes pay a higher marginal rate of tax than people with large incomes

d. all people with incomes above £1,000 per year pay the same marginal rate of tax

318

Income (£)	Amount taken by a tax (£)
7,000	800
5,000	500
3,000	300
1,000	100

Which one of the following describes the above tax?

a. proportional

b. progressive

c. regressive

d. proportional at lower incomes, progressive at higher incomes

319 In which one of the following types of tax is the marginal rate of taxation equal to the average rate?

a. a poll tax

b. a proportional income tax

c. a progressive income tax

d. a specific import duty

320 Which one of the following statements is *false*?

a. in the last resort, how much the government spends of the national income is a political decision

b. both income tax and value-added-tax have some automatic effect in stabilising the level of aggregate demand

c. the greater the elasticity of demand for a commodity, the less will be the effect on output when an indirect tax is placed upon the commodity

d. overtime working may be discouraged when the marginal rate of tax exceeds the average rate of tax

321   Given a falling demand curve and a rising supply curve, a tax per unit of output will always result in:

    a. a higher equilibrium price and a lower quantity exchanged
    b. a lower equilibrium price and a higher quantity exchanged
    c. a higher equilibrium price and a higher quantity exchanged
    d. a lower equilibrium price and a lower quantity exchanged

322   You are given the following demand schedule for cider.

Price (pence)	Quantity demanded (bottles per day)
12	18
11	24
10	30
9	36
8	42
7	48

The supply of cider is infinitely elastic, and the current price is 9p, including a tax of 2p per bottle. The chancellor of the exchequer is reviewing the tax with the object of maximising the tax revenue he can obtain from the sale of cider. Which of the following policies should the chancellor follow?

    a. leave the tax as it is
    b. raise the tax by 1p
    c. lower the tax by 1p
    d. raise the tax by 2p

323   The price of a good will not be affected by the imposition of a tax on it if:

    a. demand is perfectly elastic
    b. demand is absolutely inelastic
    c. supply is perfectly elastic
    d. supply is absolutely inelastic

324 The burden of a selective tax will be greater for the consumer than the producer if:

a. demand is inelastic and supply is inelastic
b. demand is inelastic and supply is elastic
c. demand is elastic and supply is inelastic
d. demand is elastic and supply is elastic

325 If the demand curve for wheat were perfectly elastic, a tax on wheat would:

a. have to be borne wholly by producers of wheat
b. have to be borne wholly by consumers of wheat
c. be borne partly by both
d. result in a new equilibrium at a higher price but with a smaller quantity sold

326 A tax levied on a particular factor of production:

a. will be shifted forward to buyers if the factor supply is perfectly inelastic
b. will partly be shifted forward to buyers if the factor supply is perfectly elastic
c. will be shifted forward the more to buyers the more that any reduction in price cuts down the amount supplied
d. must always be borne by the buyers of that factor

327 When a specific selective tax per unit of a commodity is imposed the effect on the amount exchanged will be greater if:

a. demand is elastic, supply is elastic
b. demand is elastic, supply is inelastic
c. demand is inelastic, supply is elastic
d. demand is inelastic, supply is inelastic

The following demand and supply schedules for 'blodgetts' refer to questions 328 to 330.

| | Quantity (thousands per week) | |
Price (pence)	Demanded	Supplied
11	60	150
10	70	130
9	80	110
8	90	90
7	100	70
6	110	50

Assume perfectly competitive market conditions.

328 What is the equilibrium market price (in pence) for 'blodgetts'?

a. 10   *b.* 9   *c.* 8   *d.* 7

329 A tax of 3p per 'blodgett' is now placed on producers. What will be the new market equilibrium price?

a. 12   *b.* 11   *c.* 10   *d.* 9

330 This 3p tax will in effect be divided between consumers and producers so that:

a. consumers pay 2p and producers 1p
b. producers pay 2p and consumers 1p
c. both pay 1½p
d. consumers pay the whole 3p

The following information and choices refer to questions 331 to 333. The demand and supply schedules refer to the market for eggs:

Price per egg (pence)	Demanded mn.	Supplied mn.
5	45	65
4	50	60
3	55	55
2	60	50
1	65	45

a. 5p   *b.* 4p   *c.* 3p   *d.* 2p

331 What would be the equilibrium free market price?

332 What would be the price if demand increased by 10 million eggs at all prices?

333 What would the price now be if the government gave a subsidy of 2p per egg to buyers?

First statement	*Second statement*
334* Capital transfer tax is a progressive tax.	The greater the amount of capital transferred, the higher the proportion of capital is taken as tax.
335* Both income tax and VAT have some automatic effect in stabilising the level of aggregate demand.	The yield from income tax and VAT rises as national income increases.

16 THE NATIONAL INCOME

336 The best question to ask in deciding whether or not a particular transaction ought to be counted in the national income for the year is:

a. was it a money transaction which involved the purchase and sale of some commodity?

b. was it a transaction involving the purchase and sale of some consumer good or service?

c. was it a transaction involving the employment of a factor of production and so resulting in the production of some commodity or service?

d. was it the production of any good or service, whether or not a money transaction was involved?

The following information and choices refer to questions 337 and 338. All figures are in £th. mn.

Wages and salaries	38
Profits and rents	11
Payments to foreigners on assets held in UK	1
Income from foreign assets held by British residents	2
Depreciation	4

a. 58   *b.* 54
c. 50   *d.* 46

337 What is the Gross National Product?

338 What is the Net National Income?

339 I Interest paid by the National Savings Bank.
    II The profit made by the Post Office during the year.
    III The cost of petrol for running Post Office vans.
    IV Spending on advertising Post Office services.

Which of the above would be included in national income calculations?

a. I, II, III and IV   *b.* II only
c. II, III and IV   *d.* I and IV

340   I Wages received by Mr Brown from ICI.
II Dividend received by Mr Brown on his ICI shares.
III The £500 by which the house owned and lived in by Mr Brown has appreciated during the year.
IV The £600 paid to Mrs Brown by her son as nominal secretary of the private company which they jointly own.

Which of the above should be included in national income calculations?

    a. I, II and III   *b.* I and IV
    c. I only   *d.* I, II, III and IV

341   Gross national expenditure less indirect taxes, plus subsidies equals:

    a. gross national product at market prices
    b. gross national product at factor cost
    c. national income
    d. personal disposable income

The following information and choices refer to questions 342 to 344. All figures are in £th. mn and apply to a country for a given year:

Expenditure on consumer goods and services by households	37
Current expenditure by public authorities	10
Expenditure on capital goods by firms and public authorities	10
Subsidies	1
Income from abroad	2
Indirect taxes	8
Income paid abroad	1
Goods and services exported	11
Goods and services imported	12
Depreciation	4

    a. 57   *b.* 53
    c. 50   *d.* 46

342   What is Gross National Product at market prices?

343   What is Gross National Product at factor cost?

344   What is National Income?

The following choices refer to questions 345 to 347.

   a. indirect taxes – subsidies
   b. depreciation
   c. net property income from abroad
   d. transfer incomes

Complete each equation in questions 345 to 347 with one of the above choices.

345   Gross national product = gross domestic product + . . .

346   Gross national product at market prices = gross national product at factor cost + . . .

347   Gross national product = net national product + . . .

The following information and choices refer to questions 348 and 349. All figures are in £mn:

   The capital stock of a country was valued at the beginning of the year at 2,000 and at the end of the year at 2,500. Capital consumption during the year was 100.

   a. 800   *b.* 700
   c. 600   *d.* 500

348   What was gross investment?

349   What was net investment?

350   The elimination of double counting means that in National Income or Gross National Product calculations we measure only the value of:

   a. all business and consumer goods purchased
   b. all sales receipts of firms producing consumer goods, and all the sales receipts of firms buying producers' goods
   c. total firms' sales at each stage of production
   d. actual production during a year whether the goods are sold to consumers or retained in the hands of businessmen

351 The value of the vegetables a retired schoolmaster grows in his garden is excluded from calculations of the national income because:

a. retired persons' activities are not included in these calculations

b. the goods are not exchanged through the market mechanism

c. it would involve double counting

d. there is no way of imputing a value to such goods

352 Which one of the following would you *not* deduct from national income in calculating personal disposable income?

a. direct taxes

b. national insurance contributions

c. undistributed profits

d. indirect taxes

353 Changes in the standard of living of the people of the UK would be indicated best by changes in:

a. the Index of Retail Prices

b. the Index of weekly wage-rates

c. the Index of industrial production

d. net national product per head

354 A nation's economic prosperity is best measured by:

a. its terms of trade with other countries

b. the percentage of the working population to total population

c. the amount of goods and services per person produced in a year

d. how much leisure time people have on the average

The following information refers to question 355.

	1950	1955	1960	1965	1970
National income (£mn)	8,100	8,800	10,000	13,000	16,500
Population (mn)	9	9	10	11	12
Index of Retail Prices	95	100	100	110	125

355 During which period did the country have the highest rate of growth?

a. 1950–55   b. 1955–60

c. 1960–65   d. 1965–70

First statement	Second statement
356* Gross National Product at market prices differs from Gross National Product at factor cost.	In order to convert Gross National Product at market prices into Gross National Product at factor cost, it is necessary to add indirect taxes and deduct subsidies.

17 THE NATURE AND CAUSES OF UNEMPLOYMENT

357 If in the UK 1 million of the working population are registered as unemployed, what percentage of unemployment does this represent?

   a. 8   *b.* 6   *c.* 4   *d.* 2

The following choices refer to questions 358 and 359.

   a. seasonal   *b.* frictional
   c. structural   *d.* cyclical

358 Which type of unemployment is likely to benefit most from a general all-round increase in government spending?

359 Which type of unemployment is likely to benefit most from subsidies given by the government to particular industries?

360 Which of the following statements is false?

   a. during the 1930s there was severe unemployment with all areas and industries experiencing approximately the same degree of unemployment

   b. unemployment of labour is particularly serious because of the human aspects

   c. export industries are particularly vulnerable to changes in the level of employment

   d. Development Area policy is principally designed to remove unemployment of a structural nature

361 If, as in the 1930s, the United Kingdom had an unemployment rate of 22 per cent which one of the following would be the *least* likely to occur?

   a. human suffering
   b. falling prices
   c. an inadequate national income
   d. a high labour turnover

362   Which of the following is the basic cause of cyclical unemployment?

  a. a general deficiency in the demand for goods and services
  b. the reluctance of workers to move to other parts of the country where there is work
  c. the inability to change occupations because of lack of the necessary skills
  d. workers' ignorance of opportunities in other occupations and districts

363   The figures for unemployment for two different countries for a given time are as follows:

	Number of vacancies (th.)	Number of unemployed (th.)
Country A	400	330
Country B	330	400

Which of the following statements is true?

  a. in country A there is a strong case for increasing aggregate demand
  b. in country A there is no need to take action over unemployment, since there are more vacancies then unemployed workers
  c. in country B the number unemployed exceeds the number of vacancies and so unemployment policy should concentrate entirely on increasing aggregate demand
  d. in country B unemployment is such that measures for increasing aggregate demand and improving the mobility of labour would both be appropriate

First statement	*Second statement*
364* The level of unemployment in the North-East Region of the UK has been persistently higher than that in the South-East Region.	The shipbuilding industry has declined whereas those industries which predominate in the South-East have mostly expanded.

18 EMPLOYMENT AND LABOUR MOBILITY

365 The figures for unemployment at a given time are:

Number of vacancies   500,000
Number of unemployed   410,000

The most likely cause of the above unemployment is:

a. a government credit squeeze
b. immobility of labour
c. a lack of aggregate demand
d. none of the above

366 I Some inefficiency in the working of the price mechanism.
II Lower wages for similar work persisting in some parts of the country compared with others.
III Higher unemployment in some areas than in others.

Which of the above are results of the immobility of labour?

a. II and III   b. I, II and III
c. I only   d. I and II

367 Which of the following is *not* an advantage of taking work to the workers?

a. it avoids uprooting workers
b. it secures the full advantages of the localisation of industry
c. it avoids further congestion of industry in the Midlands and Greater London area
d. it avoids the loss of certain social capital

368 Which of the following do you consider would be direct advantages of greater diversity of industry in coalmining and steel-producing districts?

I Less dependence on one major industry.

II Other industries would be bound to have lower costs of production.

III Demands for wage increases by workers already in the district would be reduced.

IV More work available for women.

  a. I, II, III and IV   *b.* I and III only

  c. II and IV only   *d.* I and IV only

First statement	*Second statement*
369* The price system is not fully efficient in moving labour from areas of high unemployment to areas of labour shortage.	Labour tends to be immobile.

19 CYCLICAL FLUCTUATIONS IN INCOME AND EMPLOYMENT

The following choices refer to questions 370 and 371.

a. stocks of goods held are reduced
b. additional workers are employed
c. stocks of goods held are increased
d. workers are laid off

370 In an economy where there is less than full employment, what would be the *immediate* effect of an increase in aggregate demand?

371 In an economy where there is less than full employment, what would be the *longer term* effect of an increase in aggregate demand?

372 The following unemployment figures refer to a country at a given time:

Number of vacancies	300,000
Number of unemployed	710,000

From these figures we can conclude:

I An increase in aggregate demand would be likely to reduce unemployment.
II There is scope for increasing the national output.
III Some unemployment is caused by the immobility of labour.

Which of the above statements is correct?

a. II only
b. I and II
c. I, II and III
d. III only

373 Which of the following would count as an increase in aggregate demand for purposes of estimating fluctuations in the level of national income?

I Spending by households on new colour TV sets.

II Spending by households on new Fiat cars from Italy.

III Spending by firms on additional new machines to increase output.

IV The purchase by firms of additional factory space from other firms which are going out of business.

a. I only   b. I and II only
c. I and III only   d. I, II, III and IV

The following diagram and choices refer to questions 374 to 377.

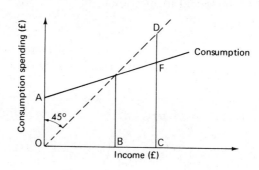

a. OA   b. OB   c. OC   d. DF

374   At what level of income will all income be spent?

375   What is the minimum consumption spending at any level of income?

376   What will be the level of saving at an income of OC?

377   If spending is FC, what will be the equilibrium level of income?

378   As a household's income increases, its consumption typically:
   a. remains the same
   b. increases by the same amount as income increases
   c. increases by more than the increase in income
   d. increases by less than the increase in income

379 In any one period, consumption spending may be greater than income for all the following reasons *except:*
 a. people spend past savings
 b. people buy on credit
 c. people borrow from the bank to spend
 d. incomes have risen more than the prices of goods

380 Which one of the following would be most likely to increase consumption spending in the short run?
 a. the government increases the initial deposit on hire purchase buying
 b. people generally become more thrifty
 c. a reduction in the level of national insurance contributions
 d. the expectation of tax reductions on goods in the budget in six months' time

381 In national income calculations, saving is defined as:
 a. that part of income not spent
 b. how much is held in a savings account
 c. that part of income held in the form of money
 d. that part of income which is lent to a bank

382 In the short run, the main factor affecting private saving in the community is:
 a. the facilities for saving offered by the government
 b. the level of income
 c. how much has to be paid on mortgages and insurance premiums
 d. the size of family

383 Which one of the following would decrease real saving in an economy?
 a. an increased budget deficit in conditions of full employment
 b. a company transfers to reserves an increase in its profits
 c. Mr Jones allocates the whole of his increase in salary to the purchase of shares in ICI
 d. Mr Jones pays higher insurance premiums to provide for a higher lump sum when he retires

384   If householders do not consume all their income but use a part of it to buy securities on the Stock Exchange, in national income terms they are:

    a. saving and investing
    b. saving but not investing
    c. investing but not saving
    d. neither saving nor investing

385   Which one of the following would an economist include as 'investment spending' for purposes of national income calculations?

    a. Mr Jones puts £50 in the National Savings Bank
    b. Mr Jones spends £500 on a new issue of Dunlop shares
    c. Mr Jones buys a 20-year-old house
    d. a supermarket spends £5,000 on increasing its stock-holding

386   Which one of the following is most likely to lead to an increase in the level of investment?

    a. a small rise in the rate of interest
    b. an increase in the level of unemployment
    c. improved profit expectations of entrepreneurs
    d. a fall in the general level of prices

The following choices refer to questions 387 to 392.

    a. 120   *b.* 100   *c.* 80   *d.* 20

For these questions assume that:

  (i) there is no excess capacity in the stainless steel sink-making industry;

  (ii) there is the capacity to produce more machines which press these sinks;

  (iii) entrepreneurs in the sink-making industry expect changes in demand to continue;

  (iv) each pressing machine can make 5,000 steel sinks a year;

  (v) the life of a machine is 5 years.

387   Assuming that demand for sinks in year 1 and previously is running at 500,000 a year, how many machines are needed to produce the sinks demanded?

388 How many machines have to be produced each year to replace those wearing out?

Now assume that in year 2 demand for sinks increases to 600,000.

389 How many machines will be required to produce this number?

390 How many machines extra to those required for normal replacement will now have to be produced by the machine-making industry?

391 By what percentage must the capacity of the machine-making industry be increased to meet this extra demand?

392 By what percentage has the demand for sinks increased between year 1 and year 2?

393 Given certain assumptions, the accelerator principle shows that:

a. consumption and investment are negatively related
b. a change in consumption produces a smaller proportionate change in investment
c. a change in consumption produces the same proportionate change in investment
d. unless the rate of increase of consumption is maintained the previous level of investment may not be maintained

394 The marginal propensity to consume is:

a. the proportion of income spent on consumption
b. the proportion of any addition to income which is not saved
c. the level of consumption relative to total income
d. the desire of people to consume at any particular level of income

395 If the marginal propensity to consume is 0·8, then the marginal propensity to save must be:

a. 0·1   *b.* 0·2
c. 0·3   *d.* 0·4

396   You are given the following table:

Total income (£)	Total amount saved (£)
400	0
600	30
800	50
1,000	100

What is the marginal propensity to consume between £800 and £1,000 income?

   a. 0·9   *b.* 0·85

   c. 0·80   *d.* 0·75

397   The multiplier shows by how much:

   a. an increase in income increases consumption

   b. a decrease in saving decreases income

   c. an increase in income increases investment

   d. a decrease in investment decreases income

398   Which one of the following is the size of the multiplier when the marginal propensity to consume is 0·8?

   a. 2   *b.* 5

   c. 8   *d.* 10

399   In a closed economy with no government, an increase in intended saving will result in:

   a. an increase in investment equal to the increase in saving

   b. a fall in investment equal to the increase in saving

   c. a fall in consumption which will reduce the level of income

   d. a fall in income equal to the increase in saving

400   If there is less than full employment, an increase in the level of investment at all levels of income:

   a. is bound to lead to an increase in income

   b. will lead to an increase in income only if the marginal propensity to consume is less than one

   c. will lead to an increase in income only if the marginal propensity to consume is diminishing

   d. will lead to an increase in income only if the marginal propensity to consume is not diminishing

401 If there is less than full employment and income expands as a result of an increase in investment, it is reasonable to expect:

    a. consumption to rise, but saving to fall
    b. both consumption and saving to rise
    c. consumption to fall, but saving to rise
    d. neither consumption nor saving to change

402 If there is less than full employment and originally income is in equilibrium, the result of an increase in investment is likely to be:

    a. income increases, but savings remain unchanged
    b. income and savings both increase
    c. income remains unchanged, but savings increase
    d. income increases but savings decrease

403 If there is less than full employment and originally income is in equilibrium, the final result of households deciding to save a larger proportion of their income is if investment does not change:

    a. income increases, but total saving remains unchanged
    b. income and total saving both increase
    c. income falls and total saving remains unchanged
    d. income falls but total saving increases

404 If only a part of any addition to income is saved, and investment spending increases by £10 mn, it will:

    a. increase the level of income by £10 mn
    b. increase the level of income by more than £10 mn
    c. increase the level of income by less than £10 mn
    d. not alter the level of income

The following information and choices refer to questions 405 to 408. Assume that c, the proportion of income consumed, is constant at all levels of income:

    a. £10,000 mn   *b.* £15,000 mn
    c. £20,000 mn   *d.* £30,000 mn

405 What is the equilibrium level of income when $c = 0.9$ and investment spending $= £2,000$ mn?

406 What would be the new equilibrium level of income if c fell to 0·8?

407 What would be the equilibrium level of income if c remained at 0·8 but investment spending rose to £3,000 mn?

408 What would be the equilibrium level of income if investment spending remained at £3,000, but increased to 0·9?

The following information relates to questions 409 to 412. All figures are in £mn. Happyland is a country where there is no government spending or taxation, but it has trade with the rest of the world. In Happyland's economy, investment = 40, exports = 40, consumption expenditure = $\frac{9}{10}$ of income at all levels of income, imports = $\frac{1}{9}$ consumers' expenditure at all levels of income.

409 Which one of the following is the equilibrium level of Happyland's national income?
  a. 200   *b.* 400   *c.* 600   *d.* 800

410 Which one of the following represents the level of imports?
  a. 20   *b.* 30   *c.* 40   *d.* 50

411 If investment spending increased to 60 but exports remained unchanged, which one of the following would be the new equilibrium level of income?
  a. 300   *b.* 500   *c.* 700   *d.* 900

412 Which one of the following now represents the balance of payments surplus (+) or deficit (−)?
  a. + 20   *b.* + 10   *c.* − 10   *d.* − 20

413 In an open economy in which the budget is balanced, there will be an equilibrium level of income if:
  a. the amount by which private saving exceeds investment is equal to the balance of payments deficit
  b. the amount by which private saving is less than investment is equal to the balance of payments surplus
  c. saving and investment are equal, but there is a balance of payments surplus
  d. the amount by which private saving exceeds investment is equal to the balance of payments surplus

414 If there is considerable unemployment owing to lack of aggregate demand, the government should:

   a. increase taxation and lower government spending
   b. increase taxation and raise government spending
   c. leave both taxes and government spending unchanged
   d. decrease taxation and raise government spending

415 In a closed economy where there is an equilibrium level of income and saving is equal to investment, government spending must be:

   a. greater than receipts from taxation
   b. equal to receipts from taxation
   c. less than receipts from taxation
   d. equal to investment

416 Which one of the following is a reason why the downturn in the trade cycle eventually comes to an end?

   a. the marginal propensity to save increases when income falls to a low level
   b. replacement of machines cannot be postponed indefinitely
   c. both government spending and taxation fall at a low level of income
   d. imports tend to rise at low levels of income

The following diagram and choices refer to questions 417 and 418. The full employment level of income is OM.

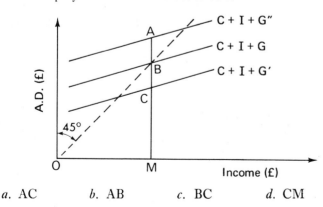

   a. AC   *b.* AB   *c.* BC   *d.* CM

417 If aggregate expenditure is represented by the curve $C + I + G''$, what is the 'inflationary gap'?

418 If aggregate expenditure is represented by the curve $C + I + G'$, what is the 'deflationary gap'?

For questions 419 to 423 assume:
 (i) investment is autonomous;
(ii) a closed economy.

419 In a closed economy, income will be at an equilibrium level if:
 a. the government has a budget surplus exactly equal to the excess of private investment over private saving
 b. the government has a budget deficit exactly equal to the excess of private investment over private saving
 c. the government has a budget surplus exactly equal to the excess of private saving over private investment
 d. the excess of private saving over private investment exactly equals government spending

420 If the economy is in equilibrium and the budget is balanced:
 a. saving must be greater than investment
 b. saving must be less than investment
 c. saving must equal investment
 d. consumption plus investment must equal the level of income

421 Assume a closed economy where the government spends (from borrowing) but does not tax. Government expenditure increases by £500 mn. If the marginal propensity to consume is 0·9, by how much has income increased when it is in equilibrium again?
 a. £500 mn   *b.* £1,000 mn
 c. £3,000 mn   *d.* £5,000 mn

The following information relates to questions 422 and 423. All figures are in £mn. Utopia is a closed economy where: investment = 200; government spending = 120; consumption = $\frac{4}{5}$ disposable income; taxation = $\frac{1}{4}$ national income (both at all levels of income). No government spending is in the form of transfer income.

422 Which one of the following represents the equilibrium level of national income?

   a. 400   *b.* 600

   c. 800   *d.* 1,000

423 Which one of the following represents the budget surplus (+) or deficit (−)?

   a. +80   *b.* +40

   c. −40   *d.* −80

424 Other things being equal, if there is less than full employment, which of the following changes is likely to improve the situation?

   a. a reduction in family allowances
   b. an increase in imports
   c. an increase in government spending
   d. a National Savings campaign

425 The present level of a country's national income is £19,000 mn, whereas it is estimated that the full employment level is £20,000 mn. The government proposes, without changing taxation, to increase its spending through a public works programme by £1,000 mn. Assuming people save only a part of any increase in income, this spending will be:

   a. just right
   b. too much
   c. not enough
   d. irrelevant to what is really required

First statement	*Second statement*
426* The upturn to a cyclical depression may occur spontaneously without government intervention.	At the bottom of a depression the marginal propensity to consume is likely to be high and any increase in investment will therefore lead to a correspondingly larger increase in income.

20 THE NATURE OF INTERNATIONAL TRADE

427 I Different countries have different tastes.

II Factors of production are not easily transferred between different countries.

III Factors of production are not evenly distributed between countries.

Which of the above conditions are necessary for international trade to take place?

   a. I only   *b.* III only

   c. II and III   *d.* I and II

428 Which one of the following statements is true?

   a. the differences between trade between countries and trade between regions within a country originate basically in political rather than economic causes

   b. the law of comparative costs explains the pattern and volume of international trade

   c. a country will always specialise completely in producing that good in which it has the greatest relative advantage

   d. countries will tend to specialise as long as the opportunity cost of obtaining a good from the international market is less than the opportunity cost of obtaining that good by its own production

For questions 429 to 435, assume the following conditions:

  (i) the cost of producing a commodity (in terms of opportunity cost) remains constant at all levels of output;

  (ii) there are no restrictions to free trade;

  (iii) there are no transport costs.

429 Two countries, Happyland and Utopia, produce only machines and tea as follows:

Country	Output per unit of factors used machines	tea
Happyland	1	2
Utopia	2	5

Which of the following is true?

  a. no trade can take place between them
  b. if trade takes place, Happyland will produce tea
  c. if trade takes place Utopia will produce both tea and machines
  d. if trade takes place, each country will produce one good and none of the other

430 A country engaged in international trade will tend to export those goods which:

  a. are produced by those factors with which it is most plentifully endowed
  b. are not subject to the import duties of other countries
  c. earn the greatest profit in foreign markets
  d. are not produced by other countries

431 Possible gains from international trade are:

  a. the advantages of specialisation can be obtained
  b. increased competition
  c. more scope for the economies of large-scale production
  d. all the above

432 I The law of comparative costs shows how countries can benefit by specialising and trading in those goods in which they have the greatest relative advantage.
  II The law of comparative costs shows that if one country is better at producing every good than another country no international trade can take place between them.

Which of the above statements is true?

  a. Neither   *b.* I only
  c. II only   *d.* I and II

433   If two countries, X and Y, divide their factors of production equally between producing machines and tea, their output is:

Country	Machines	Tea
X	200	2,000
Y	1,400	2,400

This schedule suggests a strong possibility that both countries will be better off if:

    a. X specialises in producing machines, and Y tea
    b. X specialises in producing tea and Y machines
    c. each country produces both machines and tea
    d. X specialises in producing tea, but Y produces both tea and machines

434   I The amount of goods a nation can produce in a given period is limited by its productive resources.

II Specialisation in international trade enables a nation to enjoy more goods and services than it could if it relied solely on its own efforts.

III If country A has an absolute advantage over country B in producing good X, and country B has an absolute advantage over country A in producing good Y, trade is bound to take place between them.

Which of the above statements is true?

    a. I, II, III   *b.* I only
    c. I and II   *d.* II only

435   With their factors of production, two countries, A and B, can produce units of wheat and cloth as follows:

Country A	16 wheat or 2 cloth
Country B	8 wheat or 4 cloth

Assuming constant costs of production and no transport costs or restrictions on trade, we can conclude:

    a. country A will export wheat and import cloth
    b. country B will import cloth and export wheat
    c. country A will export cloth and import wheat
    d. the exact pattern of trade cannot be determined from the above information

436 The terms of trade are defined as:
  a. the degree of competition existing in international trade
  b. the difference between exports and imports
  c. the difference in value between exports and imports
  d. the rate at which exports exchange for imports

The following information and choices refer to questions 437 and 438. Utopia, which calculates its terms of trade in the same way as the UK, has the following figures:

Year	Index of export prices	Index of import prices
1974	100	100
1975	95	100
1976	121	110

  a. 95   *b.* 100   *c.* 105   *d.* 110

437 What are Utopia's terms of trade in 1975?

438 What are Utopia's terms of trade in 1976?

439 With a unit of factors of production costing £1 sterling, the UK can produce 3 machines or 3 cars. With the same given unit of factors of production costing $1, the USA can produce 8 machines or 4 cars. If cars and machines were the only commodities entering into international trade, the UK and the USA could trade profitably:
  a. at any exchange rate because there is a difference in comparative costs
  b. if the exchange rate was such that 3 machines could be exchanged for 2 cars
  c. if the exchange rate was such that 2 machines could be exchanged for 3 cars
  d. at no rate of exchange

440 Other things being equal, which of the following changes would be most likely to improve Britain's terms of trade?
  a. a rise in world coffee prices
  b. underdeveloped countries increase their own demand for raw materials
  c. a large increase in world demand for British cars
  d. increased Japanese competition in foreign markets

The following information refers to questions 441 to 443. Assume that originally Britain obtains all her oil supplies from Bahrein. Now imagine that a large oil well is discovered in the North Sea which can be connected by a pipe-line and supply all Britain's oil requirements.

441 As a result of this discovery:

a. the world price of oil will tend to fall and the quantity exchanged internationally will increase

b. the price of oil will rise and the quantity exchanged will decrease

c. the price of oil will rise and the quantity exchanged will increase

d. the price of oil will fall and the quantity exchanged will decrease

442 If there is no other change in the prices of goods exchanged internationally, Britain's terms of trade will be:

a. improved

b. worsened

c. unchanged

d. improved in some circumstances, worsened in others

443 The following statements can be made about the effect on real income:

I A rise on the average for people in Britain.

II A rise on the average for people in Bahrein.

III A rise below the average for British shareholders in shipping companies with oil tanker fleets.

IV A fall on the average for people in Bahrein.

Which of the above statements is true?

a. I only   *b.* I and IV   *c.* I, III, IV   *d.* IV only

444 Which one of the following reasons for imposing a tariff would be most difficult to justify on economic grounds?

a. a country has a balance of payments deficit

b. there is unemployment in home based industries producing the same goods

c. the goods are produced by foreign workers on low wage rates

d. help should be given to the home industry in its infancy

Questions 445 and 446 are based on the following choices:
  a. specific tariffs
  b. ad valorem duties
  c. quotas in terms of money
  d. quotas in terms of volume

445 If prices rise, which would give the greatest degree of protection compared with previously?

446 If prices rise, which will give the least degree of protection compared with previously?

447 Which one of the following organisations is most directly concerned with freeing international trade generally?
  a. the General Agreement on Tariffs and Trade (GATT)
  b. the Sterling Area
  c. the European Economic Community (EEC)
  d. the North Atlantic Treaty Organisation (NATO)

	First statement	*Second statement*
448*	The theory of comparative costs merely shows the possibilities of increased production through specialisation.	The actual pattern of trade between two countries depends upon relative demand for goods in addition to comparative costs.

21 THE BALANCE OF PAYMENTS

449 The balance of payments of the United Kingdom records:

    a. all the assets and liabilities of all residents of the UK
    b. for residents of the UK, all payments to and receipts from residents outside the UK
    c. for the Government of the UK, only the payments to and receipts from foreign governments
    d. only payments for imports and receipts from exports

450 Other things being equal, which one of the following would lead to Britain spending dollars?

    a. British Leyland cars are sold to an American distributor
    b. an American tourist stays at an hotel in London
    c. America spends more in maintaining her base at Holy Loch
    d. the General Accident Company of Britain loses on its American insurance business

451 Other things being equal, which one of the following would lead to Britain earning dollars?

    a. a British ship refuels in the USA
    b. American shareholders in British Leyland are paid a dividend
    c. British Airways buys the Jumbo jet
    d. Bob Hope travels to Britain in the *Queen Elizabeth 2*

452 The 'visible balance' (the balance of trade) is:

    a. the difference between imports and exports
    b. the rate at which exports exchange for imports
    c. the difference in value between services rendered abroad and services obtained from abroad
    d. the difference in value between exports and imports

453 Even though Britain could not increase the value of her exports, she could still, other things being equal, import more in value from abroad by:

a. raising import duties on foreign goods
b. encouraging more tourists to visit Britain
c. increasing her aid to under-developed countries
d. increasing her gold and foreign currency reserves

454 Given that the UK wishes to maintain her existing exchange rate, which one of the following would be the most likely indication that she has a balance of payments deficit?

a. the Exchange Equalisation Account is selling convertible currency on the foreign exchange market
b. the Exchange Equalisation Account is buying convertible currency on the foreign exchange market
c. the UK is lending abroad on a short-term basis
d. the UK's imports exceed her exports in value

455 If a nation's balance of international payments shows that the value of its imports plus its long-term capital outflows are equal in value to its exports, the nation has:

a. a balance of payments equilibrium
b. a 'visible balance' surplus
c. a 'visible balance' deficit
d. a 'current balance' deficit

The following information refers to questions 456 to 462. During a given year country X records the following transactions (£mn net) with the rest of the world:

I	value of imports	100
II	value of exports	200
III	receipts from shipping	200
IV	spending by citizens travelling abroad	100
V	government expenditure abroad	100
VI	interest from overseas investments	100
VII	long-term investment abroad	100

456 Which of the above items would come under the heading of 'visible balance'?

    a. I, II, VII   *b.* III only
    c. I and II   *d.* I, II and III

457 Which of the above items are 'invisibles'?

    a. III, IV, V and VI   *b.* III, IV, V, VI and VII
    c. IV only   *d.* VI and VII

458 Which of the above items represent capital flows?

    a. IV, V, VI and VII   *b.* V, VI and VII
    c. VI and VII   *d.* VII only

The following choices refer to questions 459 to 462.

    a. + 200   *b.* + 100
    c. − 100   *d.* − 200

459 What is the visible balance?

460 What is the current balance?

461 What is the total currency flow?

462 If country X repaid £200 mn to the International Monetary Fund and had no other transactions, what was the change in her gold and convertible currency reserves (addition −, loss +)?

	First statement	*Second statement*
463*	The UK would be in a better position to give aid to under-developed countries if it had a balance of payments surplus.	A balance of payments surplus means that receipts from visible exports exceeds payments for visible imports.

22 FOREIGN EXCHANGE RATES

The following information and choices refer to questions 464 and 465. Assume a freely fluctuating foreign exchange market with the demand for and the supply of sterling in the market on a certain day as follows:

Price of sterling in US dollars	1·5	1·6	1·7	1·8	1·9
£mn demanded per day	50	40	35	30	25
£mn supplied per day	25	30	35	45	55

a. 1·5 dollars   b. 1·6 dollars
c. 1·7 dollars   d. 1·8 dollars

464 How many dollars will the £ sterling exchange for when the market is in equilibrium?

465 Suppose there is a flight of hot money from London so that the demand for sterling decreased by £10 mn at *all* prices. What would be the new rate at which dollars exchange for £ sterling?

The following information refers to questions 466 and 467. Assume that there is a system of freely fluctuating exchange rates and that 6 months ago £1 sterling exchanged for 1·70 dollars. Today the exchange rate is 1·60 dollars.

466 Which one of the following is likely to have brought about this change?
    a. an increase in the value of USA's exports to the UK but no increase in UK's exports to the USA
    b. an increase in the value of the UK's exports to the USA but no increase in USA's exports to the UK
    c. a large increase in the number of American visitors to the UK
    d. a considerable increase in spending by the USA on its forces based in Britain

467 What would be the immediate effect of this change?
    a. British goods are now less expensive for USA consumers
    b. British goods are now more expensive for USA consumers

    c. USA goods are now less expensive for British consumers

    d. none of the above

468   Other things being equal, which one of the following would be likely to cause the £ to appreciate in terms of the dollar?

    a. short-term capital moves from New York to London following a rise in the UK bank rate

    b. ICI buys an American company with funds raised on the London market

    c. UK citizens spend more in the USA and US visitors to Britain spend less

    d. the UK repays a loan to the USA

469   Assume that the Exchange Equalisation Account wishes to maintain the external value of the £ sterling. Which one of the following would tend to lead to the Account's buying sterling?

    a. a large increase in the value of British exports

    b. a large increase in the value of Britain's imports

    c. Germany agrees to offset much of the cost of stationing British troops on the Rhine

    d. a movement of hot money into London

The following diagram and choices refer to questions 470 and 471.

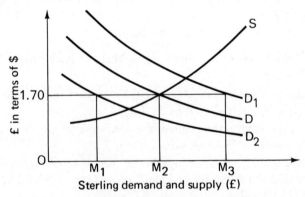

Curves D and S represent the original conditions of demand and supply respectively of sterling in the foreign exchange market.

The Exchange Equalisation Account is maintaining the rate at $1·70 to £1 sterling.

a. sell M_2M_3 sterling   b. buy M_2M_3 sterling
c. buy M_1M_2 sterling   d. sell M_1M_2 sterling

470 What action will the Account take if demand moves to D_1?

471 What action will the Account take if demand moves to D_2?

472 A British firm is sending Mr Jones to take charge of its office in New York. In the UK he is earning £5,000 per annum. It is thought that an increase in his salary of 20 per cent is justified. The rate of exchange is $1·70 to £1 sterling. The firm agrees to give him $10,200 per annum. You are asked to advise on the above arrangement:

a. it is satisfactory because a 20 per cent salary increase is a very good rise
b. it is satisfactory because the exchange rate between two currencies adequately reflects differences in their price levels
c. it is unsatisfactory because the exchange rate is fixed arbitrarily by governments in agreement with the International Monetary Fund
d. it is unsatisfactory because the exchange rate may be determined by goods which hardly figure in Mr Jones' spending

First statement	*Second statement*
473* Although the UK has adopted the system of floating exchange rates, in practice the day-to-day rate at which the £ sterling exchanges is not solely determined by changes in the conditions of demand and supply in the foreign exchange market.	The Exchange Equalisation Account intervenes in the market to ensure that the exchange rate of the £ sterling will allow British exports to be price competitive.

23 THE CORRECTION OF A BALANCE OF PAYMENTS DISEQUILIBRIUM

The following information refers to questions 474 and 475. Assume there are two countries in international trade, X and Y. X has a balance of payments deficit, Y a surplus.

474 Which of the following policies would be most likely to remove the balance of payments disequilibrium?

 a. X deflates, Y inflates   *b*. X inflates, Y deflates
 c. X deflates, Y deflates   *d*. X inflates, Y inflates

475 Assuming that there is a high elasticity of demand for the exports of both countries, which of the following policies would be most likely to remove the balance of payments disequilibrium?

 a. X devalues, Y revalues   *b*. X devalues, Y devalues
 c. X revalues, Y devalues   *d*. X revalues, Y revalues

476 A declared reduction in the value at which sterling exchanges for gold and other currencies is termed:

 a. deflation   *b*. depreciation
 c. revaluation   *d*. devaluation

477 I The standard monetary unit of a country has a given exchange rate with gold.
  II Gold coins are used as a medium of exchange within the country.
  III Gold can always be purchased from the monetary authorities at the agreed rate.
  IV Gold can be imported or exported freely.

Which of the above conditions must be fulfilled for a country to be on 'the gold standard'?

 a. I and II   *b*. I only
 c. I, III and IV   *d*. I, II, III and IV

478 Under the gold standard mechanism a deficit in the balance of payments would mean that:

 a. gold leaves the country, home prices fall
 b. gold leaves the country, foreign prices fall
 c. gold comes into the country, home prices rise
 d. gold comes into the country, foreign prices rise

479 Under the gold standard mechanism, the Bank of England acted to check an outflow of gold by:

 a. raising the bank rate
 b. forbidding the export of gold
 c. devaluing sterling
 d. selling sterling on the foreign exchange market

480 Under the gold standard mechanism, when the Bank of England raised the bank rate, it tended to produce all the following results *except*:

 a. an increase in the rate of interest charged on 'call money'
 b. a reduction in the price obtained for a bill of exchange
 c. an increase in the inward flow of foreign short-term capital
 d. an increase in the number of bills discounted on the London market

481 I The home price in sterling is reduced.
  II The rate at which the £ sterling exchanges for other currencies is depreciated.

Assuming foreign demand for British exports is elastic, which of the above policies would be likely to increase earnings from exports?

 a. I only   *b.* II only
 c. I and II   *d.* neither I nor II

482 When a country devalues its currencies relative to other countries, it will:

 a. improve its terms of trade
 b. worsen its terms of trade
 c. have no effect on its terms of trade
 d. be irrelevant to its terms of trade

483   Country X has to take remedial action to remove a balance of payments deficit, either by deflation or devaluation. Which of the following conditions would be most likely to decide in favour of devaluation?

I Full employment in the economy.

II Unemployment in the economy.

III Demand of X for imports elastic.

IV Foreign demand for X's exports inelastic.

a. I, II and III   *b.* II and III
c. II only   *d.* III and IV

484   Which one of the following conditions, other things being equal, would be most favourable to devaluation as a means of improving a country's balance of payments?

a. an elastic demand for imports but an inelastic demand for exports

b. an elastic demand for imports and an elastic demand for exports

c. an inelastic demand for imports and an inelastic demand for exports

d. an inelastic demand for imports and an elastic demand for exports

The following information and choices refer to questions 485 and 486. The elasticity of demand for the exports of Utopia is 2, whereas her elasticity of demand for imports is ½. Devaluation by Utopia could have the following results:

I Export earnings rise.

II Export earnings fall.

III Spending on imports increases.

IV Spending on imports decreases.

a. I and III   *b.* I and IV
c. II and III   *d.* II and IV

485   Which of the above applies if Utopia calculates the changes in her own currency?

486   Which of the above applies if Utopia calculates the changes in terms of foreign currencies?

First statement

487* If the UK had a balance of payments deficit she could seek to increase the value of her exports to the USA by depreciating the £ sterling in terms of the dollar.

Second statement

The policy would be most effective if the demand of the USA for British exports was inelastic.

24 THE EUROPEAN ECONOMIC COMMUNITY

488 Which one of the following countries is not a member of the EEC?
- *a.* Denmark
- *b.* Norway
- *c.* Belgium
- *d.* The Irish Republic

The following refer to questions 489 to 491.
- *a.* The Commission
- *b.* The Council of Ministers
- *c.* The European Parliament
- *d.* The Economic and Social Committee

489 Which of the above puts forward policy proposals?

490 Which of the above can veto these proposals?

491 Which of the above is composed of representatives of the major parties of the parliaments of the member countries?

492 The distinguishing feature of the EEC is that the movement of goods in and out of the Common Market is based:
- *a.* entirely on the principle of comparative costs
- *b.* upon the formation of a customs union
- *c.* upon the establishment of a Free Trade Area
- *d.* upon the particular preferences of individual member countries

493 A possible advantage of the UK's membership of the EEC is:
- *a.* greater opportunities for trade according to comparative cost advantages
- *b.* a larger market for industries producing under conditions of decreasing cost
- *c.* increased competition for home-based monopolies
- *d.* all of the above

494 The principal indirect tax of the EEC is
- *a.* sales tax
- *b.* value-added tax
- *c.* wine and spirits duty
- *d.* television licences

495   International Computers Ltd is likely to benefit in particular
from Britain's membership of the EEC because:
   a. the demand for computers is increasing
   b. production takes place under conditions of decreasing cost
   and the EEC offers a wider market
   c. servicing computers from Britain can be quickly achieved by
   airlifting personnel
   d. financial backing is given by the Export Credit Guarantee
   Department of the Department of Trade

First statement	*Second statement*
496* The EEC imposes tariffs on goods of non-member countries entering the Common Market.	The EEC does nothing to interfere with the flow of goods arising from comparative cost advantages.

25 SOME CURRENT ECONOMIC PROBLEMS

497 According to the Quantity Theory of Money, if the supply of money is doubled:

　　a. total spending will double, and real national income will double

　　b. real national income will double, and prices will double

　　c. both spending and prices will increase but the amount of increase cannot be predicted

　　d. spending and prices will both double

498 In the equation $MV = PT$, the left-hand-side stands for:

　　a. the quantity of money in circulation

　　b. the volume of cash and bank deposits

　　c. total money expenditures

　　d. the sale value of output produced

499 An increase in the supply of money in the economy is *least* likely to lead to higher prices if:

　　a. there is a high level of unemployment

　　b. there is full employment

　　c. there is a low demand for money to hold

　　d. there is little increase in productivity

500 Which one of the following policies would a government be most likely to follow if the prices of goods in general were rising quickly and employment was at a high level?

　　a. lower the rate of interest

　　b. relax hire purchase restrictions

　　c. increase taxation without altering government spending

　　d. increase government spending without altering taxation

501 If wages increase, but the cost of living increases at a faster rate, what happens to real wages?

　　a. they are higher than before 　　*b.* they are the same as before

　　c. they are lower than before 　　*d.* they are not affected

502 One reason for inflation when there is full employment is:

a. a higher amount is raised by taxation
b. trade unions exert pressure for higher wages
c. government spending rises as prices rise
d. imports increase

503 A major defect of a prices and incomes policy is:

a. by imposing rigid prices it interferes with the allocative mechanism of the price system
b. it does not reduce imports
c. it leads to unemployment
d. it weakens trade union power in wage negotiations

504 In order to remedy a continuous rise in prices, which of the following policies would be appropriate?

I Increasing the percentage deposits in hire purchase agreements.
II Increasing the maximum repayment period in hire purchase agreements.

a. I only
b. II only
c. both I and II
d. neither I nor II

505 During times of rising prices, one way of reducing prices would be to:

a. increase the available supply of goods
b. lower the interest rate on bank loans
c. decrease personal income tax
d. increase government expenditure

506 Which of the following policies would be most appropriate to controlling a wage–cost inflation?

a. reduce the subsidies on food
b. a reduction in income tax
c. limiting wage-increases to increases in productivity
d. letting prices rise to reduce real incomes

507 The government is trying to stop a general rise in prices by a prices and incomes policy. During the year, all labour managed to secure a 10 per cent increase in wages, but productivity per man also increased 10 per cent. All other costs remain unchanged. In these circumstances the government should:

    a. allow prices to rise by 10 per cent
    b. insist on price reductions
    c. allow no average price rise whatsoever
    d. allow a price rise between 0 and 10 per cent

508 Which one of the following is the main reason for Britain's balance of payments difficulties since the war?

    a. unemployment
    b. insufficient spending by Britain on imports
    c. rising prices of imports
    d. rising prices in the UK

509 There is full employment in the British economy, but, because of a serious adverse balance of payments, she decides to devalue. At the same time deflationary measures are taken. These policies show that the government:

    a. is prepared to have unemployment in order to correct the balance of payments
    b. does not want inflation to jeopardise the benefits of devaluation
    c. does not want devaluation to lead to unemployment
    d. does not consider there is any link between devaluation and inflation

510 Which one of the following would be least favourable to growth in the UK economy?

    a. an improvement in the terms of trade
    b. a persistent deficit in the balance of payments
    c. an increase in investment in capital goods
    d. natural gas is discovered in the North Sea

511 Which one of the following could be regarded as the most satisfactory and realistic rate of growth for which the UK should aim?

a. 1 per cent   b. 3 per cent
c. 6 per cent   d. 10 per cent

The following information and choices refer to questions 512 and 513. A country produces only one product – food. Its total output (million tons) for different levels of its population is shown in the following table:

Population (mn)	Output of food
20	100
30	160
40	220
50	300
60	350

a. 30 mn   b. 40 mn
c. 50 mn   d. 60 mn

512 What is its optimum population?

513 If the population increased by 20 per cent but its capacity to produce food increased by 40 per cent, what would be its optimum population?

First statement	*Second statement*
514* If there is unemployment and the government adopts reflationary measures, the general level of prices does not start to rise until all factors are fully employed.	When there is full employment, any increase in aggregate monetary demand is likely to be inflationary.
515* Following the increase in oil prices in 1973 and 1974 economic depression occurred in the Western oil-importing countries.	The oil-exporting countries do not fully spend on imports their increase in oil revenues.

516* When there is full employment, the rate of growth can be increased by reducing current consumption.

Reducing current consumption in conditions of full employment releases resources for the production of capital goods.

517* Projections of the size of the UK's population in the year 2000 have been consistently revised downwards over the past two decades.

The UK's birth rate and average number of children per family have both fallen compared with the estimates upon which earlier projections were based.

518* The standard of living of under-developed countries can be improved by the removal of import restrictions imposed on their manufactured goods by more advanced countries.

Freer trade would enable under-developed countries to secure the comparative cost advantage of cheap labour.

ANSWERS

1–d	41–b	81–b	121–d	161–b	201–d
2–a	42–a	82–c	122–b	162–c	202–c
3–c	43–a	83–b	123–c	163–c	203–d
4–c	44–d	84–a	124–d	164–b	204–c
5–d	45–b	85–b	125–a	165–a	205–c
6–a	46–c	86–b	126–d	166–b	206–a
7–c	47–a	87–d	127–b	167–d	207–c
8–d	48–c	88–a	128–c	168–a	208–c
9–c	49–c	89–a	129–d	169–b	209–c
10–d	50–c	90–d	130–b	170–d	210–a
11–b	51–c	91–d	131–a	171–d	211–a
12–c	52–b	92–a	132–d	172–a	212–d
13–c	53–a	93–d	133–b	173–a	213–a
14–b	54–c	94–b	134–c	174–a	214–b
15–c	55–c	95–d	135–a	175–c	215–d
16–c	56–b	96–b	136–b	176–d	216–b
17–c	57–d	97–b	137–c	177–b	217–a
18–a	58–a	98–c	138–b	178–a	218–b
19–a	59–c	99–c	139–b	179–b	219–b
20–c	60–c	100–a	140–d	180–c	220–c
21–d	61–b	101–a	141–b	181–a	221–a
22–a	62–a	102–c	142–d	182–b	222–b
23–b	63–c	103–a	143–a	183–d	223–c
24–c	64–b	104–a	144–c	184–b	224–d
25–d	65–b	105–a	145–a	185–c	225–a
26–a	66–c	106–a	146–b	186–c	226–b
27–d	67–a	107–d	147–d	187–a	227–d
28–d	68–b	108–d	148–a	188–d	228–a
29–b	69–b	109–d	149–d	189–b	229–a
30–c	70–d	110–b	150–b	190–c	230–c
31–a	71–d	111–d	151–d	191–d	231–c
32–c	72–b	112–d	152–c	192–c	232–d
33–d	73–a	113–c	153–b	193–d	233–b
34–a	74–c	114–d	154–d	194–c	234–c
35–c	75–d	115–d	155–d	195–b	235–b
36–b	76–c	116–a	156–a	196–d	236–c
37–b	77–b	117–b	157–a	197–c	237–d
38–c	78–a	118–c	158–b	198–b	238–b
39–b	79–c	119–c	159–d	199–d	239–d
40–a	80–c	120–c	160–a	200–d	240–c

241–d	288–d	335–a	381–a	427–c	473–a
242–c	289–c	336–c	382–b	428–d	474–a
243–a	290–a	337–b	383–a	429–d	475–a
244–b	291–a	338–c	384–b	430–c	476–d
245–b	292–b	339–b	385–d	431–d	477–c
246–d	293–c	340–b	386–c	432–b	478–a
247–c	294–b	341–b	387–b	433–b	479–a
248–d	295–c	342–a	388–d	434–c	480–d
249–c	296–b	343–c	389–a	435–d	481–c
250–b	297–d	344–d	390–d	436–d	482–b
251–a	298–a	345–c	391–b	437–a	483–b
252–d	299–c	346–a	392–d	438–d	484–b
253–a	300–b	347–b	393–d	439–b	485–a
254–d	301–b	348–c	394–b	440–c	486–b
255–b	302–b	349–d	395–b	441–a	487–a
256–d	303–c	350–d	396–a	442–a	488–b
257–c	304–c	351–b	397–d	443–c	489–a
258–d	305–d	352–d	398–b	444–c	490–b
259–b	306–b	353–d	399–c	445–c	491–c
260–b	307–a	354–c	400–a	446–a	492–b
261–d	308–c	355–c	401–b	447–a	493–d
262–c	309–c	356–c	402–b	448–a	494–b
263–d	310–b	357–c	403–c	449–b	495–b
264–c	311–d	358–d	404–b	450–d	496–c
265–b	312–c	359–c	405–c	451–d	497–d
266–d	313–b	360–a	406–a	452–d	498–c
267–b	314–d	361–d	407–b	453–b	499–a
268–c	315–a	362–a	408–d	454–a	500–c
269–a	316–c	363–d	409–b	455–b	501–c
270–a	317–d	364–a	410–c	456–c	502–b
271–b	318–d	365–b	411–b	457–a	503–a
272–b	319–b	366–b	412–c	458–d	504–a
273–c	320–c	367–b	413–d	459–b	505–a
274–d	321–a	368–d	414–d	460–a	506–c
275–a	322–d	369–a	415–b	461–b	507–c
276–b	323–d	370–a	416–b	462–b	508–d
277–b	324–b	371–b	417–b	463–c	509–b
278–d	325–d	372–c	418–c	464–c	510–b
279–c	326–b	373–c	419–a	465–b	511–b
280–d	327–a	374–b	420–c	466–a	512–c
281–a	328–c	375–a	421–d	467–a	513–d
282–c	329–c	376–d	422–c	468–a	514–d
283–a	330–a	377–c	423–a	469–b	515–a
284–c	331–c	378–d	424–c	470–a	516–a
285–b	332–b	379–d	425–b	471–c	517–a
286–b	333–c	380–c	426–a	472–d	518–a
287–d	334–a